Duquesne Studies

LANGUAGE AND LITERATURE SERIES

Volume Nineteen

General Editor:
Albert C. Labriola

Advisory Editor:
Foster Provost

Editorial Board:
Judith H. Anderson
Donald Cheney
Ann Baynes Coiro
Mary T. Crane
Patrick Cullen
A. C. Hamilton
Margaret P. Hannay
A. Kent Hieatt
William B. Hunter
Michael Lieb
Thomas P. Roche, Jr.
Mary Beth Rose
John M. Steadman
Humphrey Tonkin
Susanne Woods

The Melancholy Muse

The *Melancholy Muse*

Chaucer, Shakespeare and Early Medicine

Carol Falvo Heffernan

DUQUESNE UNIVERSITY PRESS
Pittsburgh, Pennsylvania

Published in the United States of America by

DUQUESNE UNIVERSITY PRESS
600 Forbes Avenue
Pittsburgh, Pennsylvania 15282–0101

Library of Congress Cataloging-in-Publication Data

Heffernan, Carol Falvo.
    The melancholy muse : Chaucer, Shakespeare, and early medicine /
by Carol Falvo Heffernan.
      p. cm. — (Duquesne studies. Language and literature series
; v. 19)
    Includes bibliographical references and index.
    ISBN 0-8207-0262-5
    1. Chaucer, Geoffrey, d. 1400—Knowledge—Medicine.
2. Shakespeare, William, 1564-1616—Knowledge—Medicine.
3. Depression, Mental, in literature. 4. Chaucer, Geoffrey, d.
1400—Knowledge—Psychology. 5. Shakespeare, William, 1564-1616
—Knowledge—Psychology. 6. Literature and medicine—England
—History. 7. Lovesickness in literature. 8. Physicians in
literature. 9. Melancholy in literature. 10. Sadness in
literature. I. Title. II. Series.
    PR1933.M4H44 1995
    820.9'356—dc20

95-4368
CIP

To Geoffrey

Contents

ACKNOWLEDGMENTS

I am grateful to Rutgers University for gifts of time and money. The Research Council provided a generous grant, enabling me to purchase microfilm and photostats of many unpublished manuscripts and incunabula of ancient, medieval and Renaissance medical treatises. That started me on my way. A series of small grants from The Graduate School at Rutgers University-Newark enabled me to continue locating and reading these rare texts over a period of several years. An initial year's leave from teaching duties gave me the opportunity to begin correlating the medical views of melancholy with those in poetic works by Chaucer and Shakespeare. Later, a semester's leave gave me the time to revise the final draft of this book.

It would be hard to pinpoint when my interest in the subject of melancholy began. Surely it was vestigial in the examination of withdrawal and isolation, images of which are studied in my recent book about the handling of the phoenix myth in two poems, the "Carmen de Ave Phoenice" by the church father, Lactantius, and the Old English "Phoenix" by an anonymous Old English poet (*The Phoenix at the Fountain*, University of Delaware Press, 1988). It took clear shape in an article on Chaucer's *Book of the Duchess* and *melancholia canina* (*Modern Philology*, 1986). A number of scholarly audiences served as testing grounds for ideas that shaped themselves gradually into the chapters of this book. Early versions of chapter 2, "Chaucer's *Book of the Duchess* and the Medieval Physicians," were presented at the Twenty-third International Congress on Medieval Studies, Western Michigan University (Kalamazoo, Michigan) in May 1988, at the Sixth Congress of the International Courtly Literature Society, l'Università degli Studi di Salerno, Istituto de Linguistica (Salerno, Italy) in July 1989, to undergraduate Chaucer students at the University of Sheffield (England) in November 1990, and to graduate students in English at Rutgers University in May 1991. An early draft of chapter 3, "Chaucer's *Troilus and Criseyde*: Courtly Love and the Disease of Love," was read at the Twenty-second International Congress on Medieval Studies (Western Michigan University) in May 1987 and later appeared in *Neophilologus* (1990, 74: 294–309). Thanks are due to that journal for permission to reprint a revised version in this book. A small section of chapter 5, "*Hamlet:* Shakespeare, Melancholy, and the Renaissance Physicians," concerned with new evidence for the influence of André Du Laurens on Shakespeare, was presented at the Twelfth International Conference on Patristics, Medieval, and Renaissance Studies, The Augustinian Historical Institute, Villanova University, October 1987. Some of the ideas in this chapter that focus on Hamlet's anger were initially presented as a paper in 1989 at the Central Renaissance Conference at the University of Missouri, Kansas City. Discussions, conversations, and sometimes letter exchanges that followed these presentations were helpful in clarifying ideas. In this connection, I wish to thank to Dr. Philip Teigen, Deputy Chief Librarian of the Historical Collection at the National Medical Library, Bethesda, Maryland; Professor Laurel Braswell-Means of McMaster University; Professor Charles A. Owen, Jr. of the University of Connecticut (Storrs); Professor John Fyler of Tufts University; and Dr. Faye Getz of the University of Wisconsin (Madison).

My research was facilitated by the kind attention of many librarians at the numerous collections that welcomed me. Apart from Dr. Teigen, I wish to express my gratitude for help given me by many other librarians: the late Sallie Morgenstern, Curator of the New York Academy of Medicine's Rare Book Room, her successor, Ann Pasquale, as well as Inge Dupont, Amanda Hagerty, and Florie Berger; Jack Eckert, Curator of Archives and Manuscripts of the Library of the College of Physicians of Philadelphia; J. Conway, Superintendent, Manuscript Collections of the British Library; Muriel McCarthy of Archbishop Marsh's Library, Dublin, Ireland; J. T. D. Hall, Deputy Librarian, Cambridge University Library; and many librarians who assisted me at the Newberry Library in Chicago, the New York Public Library, and the libraries of Rutgers University.

For help in conversation or letters about specific manuscript problems or bibliographical matters, I owe thanks to Sir Charles A. Talbot, the late Professor Rossell Hope Robbins, and Professor Linda Voigts. My colleague, Ann C. Watts, read the chapter on *The Book of the Duchess* and offered helpful suggestions, as did Professor John B. Friedman, who read the entire manuscript. I also wish to thank Professor Donald Beecher, a consultant reader for Duquesne University Press, for his thorough reading of my manuscript and his constructive criticism. The final draft of the book benefited as well from the care Duquesne's senior editor, Susan Wadsworth-Booth, lavished on it, and I am also happy to acknowledge the interest shown in this study by Dr. Albert C. Labriola, general editor of the *Language and Literature Series*, and by John Dowds, the director of the Press. Grateful thanks are due as well to my husband, Tom, for his ready encouragement, intellectual stimulation and helpful advice.

Evident throughout the study are debts to many scholars of medieval and Renaissance literature as well as to historians of medicine. Three books, the first two fairly early studies, and the third more recent, were potent influences: *Saturn and Melancholy* by Raymond Klibansky, Erwin Panofsky and Fritz Saxl, *The Elizabethan Malady* by Lawrence Babb, and *Mystical Bedlam* by Michael MacDonald. Mary Wack's recent book-length study of Constantine's *Viaticum* and its commentaries, *Lovesickness in the Middle Ages*, has aims different from my own. She was concerned with a particular work, specifically its chapter on lovesickness (a subcategory of melancholy) and the influence it exerted. I have examined representative poems by Chaucer and plays by Shakespeare against a broad range of works on melancholy and mania. The application of literary and medical perspectives to texts by these two authors enable the reader to better understand what melancholy meant to the medieval and Renaissance worlds out of which they came. Though not primarily concerned with melancholy, the importance of two influential books which ventured into the uncharted waters of early medical prose should be acknowledged as well: Michel Foucault's *Madness and Civilization* and Penelope Doob's *Nebuchadnezzar's Children: Conventions of Madness in Middle English Literature*.

ONE

Melancholy—Its Background In Early Medical Texts

What Can The Poets Know?

M elancholy justifies itself as a subject for study, even on its own, as everyone can expect to feel down, blue, moody or sad some time or other. Such feelings, however, do not necessarily indicate *melancholy* or *depression*, though they are among its clinical symptoms. These responses are simply part of the normal repertoire of affective reactions to life's disappointments and losses. Dejection is so much a part of human experience that both medical and literary treatments of it abound, and these are worthy of examination both separately and together. Any attempt to understand how this body of ideas appears in literary treatments of melancholy must necessarily start with an overview of a wide range of medical sources, as most of these are unfamiliar today, difficult of access, and known only to the specialist, while they were taken for granted in their own day, when they formed part of the contemporary scene, scholarly and popular.

The following discussion is neither a medical history nor a catalog of melancholy characters in English literature; I consider the medical tradition an important aspect of the historical background that will help the reader situate imaginative treatments of melancholy within the context of the author's world. Knowledge of the medical picture can also help us appreciate more fully the literary merit of the poet's artistic treatment of melancholy. How much is invention? What is borrowed? It comes as no surprise to find that in its clinical dimension—expressed in the medical literature as signs, symptoms and cures—dejection has been written about by physicians for hundreds of years, from antiquity into the twentieth century. As a mood, emotion, expression of disappointment over some loss, and even as disease, melancholy is so pervasive an aspect of our humanity that it is further unsurprising to discover that the poetry of those two most human and important English authors, Chaucer and Shakespeare, is rich in expression of it. I select from their works—not from Coleridge or Wordsworth, Milton, Langland, or even Hoccleve—not merely because Chaucer and Shakespeare are poets worth pondering (so are the rest) but because I know them best after years of teaching and writing about their works. Moreover, they share the same inherited intellectual tradition. Others might justify studying other poets from other periods in a similar fashion.

Shakespeare's depiction of the melancholy Jaques, observations made about Hamlet's behavior by the other players and himself, Chaucer's fine distinctions about the signs of mania and melancholy in his portrait of Arcite

in the *Knight's Tale*, his portrayal of the insomniac-
dreamer of *The Book of the Duchess* and his unhappy
Troilus tempt one to think that Chaucer's knowledge
may have included Galen or Constantine the African,
Bernard of Gordon or Avicenna, and Shakespeare's, some
of these plus Timothy Bright, André Du Laurens or still
others. Chaucer enhances the Doctor of Physic's authority, indicating his knowledge of the major medical
writers of the ancient and medieval world by listing their
names. There are similar lists in Dante's *Inferno* (4.139,
143–44) and Jean de Meun's *Roman de la Rose* (15959–
61). Perhaps these are mere examples of literary name-
dropping. The allusions to matters medical in Chaucer
and Shakespeare are frequently so detailed, subtle and
accurate, however, as to suggest that their knowledge of
medicine went beyond simply picking up the general
notions of their day. It is tempting to imagine a
circularity of influences moving from medieval and Renaissance medical writers, on the one hand, to their
respective contemporaries among poets such as Chaucer
and Shakespeare, on the other, and back from the poets
to the physicians in their times. What I have found, however, is that until one gets to Burton's *Anatomy of Melancholy*, essentially a "literary" work, the medical treatises cite only medical authorities. Bernard of Gordon's
references to Ovid in his *Lilium medicinae* is typical of
Bernard's use of classical poetry but a rare instance
among early medical writers.[1] This does not mean that
physicians learned nothing about humankind from poets
but merely that in technical writing they dealt exclusively with an inherited body of medical knowledge that
was passed on from generation to generation with rela-
tive consistency. If poets touched their vision over the
ages, they go unnamed. The physicians' influence on
the poets appears, however, to have been considerable,
thus reversing the situation at academic dinner parties
where the physicist may be found to converse articu-
lately about Shakespeare while the literary critic sits

speechless on the subject of nuclear physics.

How much book learning Chaucer and Shakespeare actually had of medicine is difficult to know, but by examining writings by the doctors of medicine on the subject of melancholy and placing their thoughts beside similar ones by Chaucer and Shakespeare, it may not be too much to claim that the two poets and the early medical writers who, before the advent of twentieth century psychiatry, dared to apply their vision to the observation of mental phenomena noticed some of the same things and expressed themselves with penetrating wisdom in the different modes of their separate crafts. The aim of this study is straightforward: in a study of the way melancholy is treated in the poetry of Chaucer and Shakespeare and in the medical writing of contemporary physicians, I will attempt to demonstrate that the two poets and the medieval-Renaissance physicians viewed melancholy in parallel ways. The aim may seem too modest to bother about, but a great deal needs to be learned and understood before one can claim to see what operates in apparently *obvious* parallels, especially as the medical texts are so rare and inaccessible that relatively few literary scholars have read them. As the study proceeds from chapter to chapter, the poetic texts are placed against the background of medical prose letting the latter, mostly unfamiliar to modern readers, serve as subtexts shedding light on the better known literary works. It may occasionally appear that the poets surpass the physicians in exploring the reality of melancholy by bringing to the task insight not found in any textbook. In these instances, it will be hard to know whether the source of this capacity is poetic genius, personal knowledge of the fact of melancholy itself, a deeper understanding of the medical issues, or some subtle mix of all three possibilities.

This cross-disciplinary study attempts to contribute to scholarship by fulfilling the task of the humanist historian *in bono* who, as Lee Patterson would have it in

Negotiating the Past, shows "great writers . . . simultaneously articulating the values of their time and yet rising above them" (33). From both the literary and medical points of view, the task is large and requires the definition of boundaries to enable us to achieve reasonable ends. By focusing the following chapters on Chaucer's *The Book of the Duchess* and his *Troilus and Criseyde,* and Shakespeare's *As You Like It* and *Hamlet,* it is my intent to provide a comprehensive understanding of this subject. The works are drawn from the early and late stages of each writer's career and selected for their importance as poetic treatments of melancholy, an enduring interest of both poets. The consistency of views, artistic and scientific, leave one with the impression that medieval and Renaissance poets and scientists were able to peer over one another's shoulders more easily than their counterparts today because they essentially used the same language. More capable of understanding one another's fields, perhaps, they were more likely to influence each other. The art of Chaucer and Shakespeare was such that over and over again we see them take the received knowledge of their times—and in this I include the learned as well as the popular— and transmute it poetically into views of melancholy that, while employing psychological systems of the Middle Ages and the Renaissance, retain significance in our own day. To better appreciate their understanding of melancholy it is first necessary to understand what it meant in particular terms in early thought. What body of ideas were available to use, transmute and transcend?

MELANCHOLY

The term *melancholy* derives from the Greek μέλαινα χολή (which was transliterated into Latin as *melancholia,* a synonym for *atra bilis,* black bile), and referred to "a mental disorder involving prolonged depression" (Jackson, 4).[2] An overabundance of black bile, in the theory of the four humours, was thought to be a crucial factor in the disorder of melancholy.

As a mood rather than as a disease, melancholy is not all bad. John Milton's companion poems, *L'Allegro* and *Il Penseroso*, to cite familiar examples, give voice to the two sides of the mood, *L'Allegro* opening with the words "Hence, loathed Melancholy," and *Il Penseroso* closing on the opposite sentiment, "These pleasures, Melancholy give,/And I with thee will choose to live." The quintessential English literary study of melancholy, Robert Burton's *The Anatomy of Melancholy* (1621), also calls attention to its two sides, but here we more clearly approach the disease:

> Fear and sorrow are the true characters, and inseparable companions, of most melancholy, not all, . . . for to some it is most pleasant, as to such as laugh most part; some are bold again, and free from all manner of fear and grief (Pt. I, Sec. I, member 3, subsection 1 [Jackson ed.,170]).

This was the definition going back to Avicenna and repeated by all subsequent authorities. To add to the difficulties surrounding the term, "melancholy" can refer to a natural humour, an unnatural humour, an aspect of human temperament as well as a mental disease. Moreover, the popular expression "lovesick" turns out to have a long history in both medicine and literature, giving it its own niche as a category of melancholy (love melancholy or *amor hereos*). In both medical treatises and fiction its sufferers are seen to sigh, swoon, go mad, and sometimes die.

The medical notion of black bile as the essential element in melancholy is embedded in the theory of the humours, already familiar by the end of the fifth century B.C. The idea of the four humours—blood, yellow bile, phlegm, black bile—whose balance constituted health is first set forth by Hippocrates:

> The body of man has in itself blood, phlegm, yellow bile, and black bile; these make up the nature of his body, and

through these he feels pain or enjoys health. Now he enjoys the most perfect health when these elements are duly proportioned to one another in respect of compounding power and bulk, and when they are perfectly mingled. Pain is felt when one of these elements is in defect or excess, or is isolated in the body without being compounded in the body with all the others (4:11–13).

(But, as we shall see, it was largely through Galen's writings that humours medicine was continued in the Latin West). According to the season, one of the humours predominated: sanguine "blood" increased in the spring, cold and dry melancholy gained ascendancy in autumn, phlegm prevailed in winter, and yellow bile was engendered in the summer. The four humours came to be linked in the Middle Ages and Renaissance with the Four Ages of Man, melancholy associating itself most closely with old age, as has so eloquently been explored in recent books on the ages of man by Elizabeth Sears and Mary Dove as well as in the early study, *Saturn and Melancholy*, by Erwin Panofsky, Fritz Saxl and Raymond Klibansky. Though various degrees of woe plague all ages, the particular susceptibility of old age to melancholy is well captured in a fifteenth century "Regimen of Health" cited by Sears: "In old age, there being more concerns and anxieties than in previous ages, man becomes more tiresome to himself and is filled with misery in soul and body" (6).[3] Along similar lines, in a discussion of the inescapability of melancholy's adverse effects in the last stage of life, Mary Dove cites an observation by Henry Cuffe in his account of the correspondences between the ages of man and the seasons, "Cold, dry melancholy is reserved for Saturn-influenced winter-age" (Dove, 35).[4]

The classic examination by Klibansky, Saxl and Panofsky of the philosophic tradition leading up to Albrecht Dürer's remarkable engraving, "Melancolia I," also explores the relationship between melancholy, as understood in the classical world's doctrine of the four humours, and creativity, particularly as set forth in the famous *Problem XXX, 1,* attributed to Aristotle. Suggesting Plato's idea of the inspired frenzy of which seers and poets are possessed, the Aristotelian *Problem* raises the question: "Why is it that all those who have become eminent in philosophy or politics or poetry or the arts are clearly melancholics, and some to such an extent as to be affected by the diseases caused by black bile?" (Klibanksy, Panofsky and Saxl, 18).[5] The author of the *Problem,* thinking in terms of the theory of the humours, maintains that while ordinary people all contain black bile, a minority have it in excess and are, therefore, predisposed to be melancholic by temperament and precariously gifted as a result. This excess in those so gifted works like wine, exhilarating in the right amounts, stultifying when the amounts become too great. As *Problem XXX* states, One can see that wine makes the most varied characters, by observing how it gradually changes those who drink it; for those who, to begin with, when sober, are cool and taciturn become more talkative when they have drunk just a little too much; if they drink a little more it makes them grandiloquent and boisterous and, when they proceed to action, reckless . . . very great excess enfeebles them completely and makes them as stupid as those who have been epileptic from childhood or as those who are a prey to excessive melancholy. (Klibansky *et al.,* 19–20).

Paradoxically, as the tract explains, despondency drives men to drink in an effort to escape a melancholy so intense they "are inclined to hang themselves" (27). Profound melancholy has made them so cold they seek renewed heat in wine. Mentioned in this work among extraordinary melancholics are the heroes Hercules, an epileptic who killed his children in a fit of madness, Ajax, associated with rage, blackness and heaviness in Homer's *Odyssey,* and Aristotle's teacher, Plato, as well as *his* teacher, Socrates.

Plato had written about the *furores,* that divine madness of poets, in the *Phaedrus,* but after his death there also evolved, in later antiquity, the notion of Platonic *tristitia* or sadness, a somewhat different aspect of melancholy. This sadness, along with fear, was associated with the irascible in Plato's tripartite scheme for the soul, which contained concupiscible, irascible and rational aspects, the first two parts conflicting with the third. Bennett Simon, in his study, *Mind and Madness*, cites, in this connection, the following lines in a comedy dating from the late fourth or early third century:

> Oh Plato, all you know is how to frown,
> And solemnly raise your eyebrows like a snail (232).

To return to Aristotle, however, Simon goes to the heart of the underlying theory *and* shortcoming of the Aristotelian *Problem* when he comments, "The reason such men are melancholics, of course, lies in the quantity and quality of black bile within them, not in the inner conflicts that might beset them. . . . Psychology is translated into physiology" (232). Ignoring subtle issues of such matters as shame and aggression turned inward, which the dramatist Sophocles makes part of his portrait of melancholy in *Ajax*, for example, Aristotle describes questions about the extraordinary talents yet fragile dispositions of many melancholics, the distinction between melancholic disease and melancholic nature, all in terms of the level of black bile in the body. The answer given by Klibansky, Panofsky and Saxl to the question posed at the beginning of the Aristotelian *Problem XXX, 1* is that "the amount of melancholy humour must be great enough to raise the character above the average, but not so great as to generate a melancholy 'all too deep,' and that it must maintain an average temperature between 'too hot' and 'too cold'" (32).

Acedia *and Melancholy*

Important to medieval and Renaissance artistic and medical thinking on melancholy is *acedia*, a theological concept (brilliantly studied by Siegfried Wenzel as *The Sin of Sloth*) which began as a deadly sin and evolved into a psychiatric syndrome. John Cassian (ca. A.D. 360–435), a student of St. Jerome and St. John Chrysostom, discussed *acedia* in terms of the solitary monastic life and defined it as *taedium sive anxietas cordis* (boredom or anxiety; Altschule, 117). For Cassian, anger and *acedia* were to be counted among the deadly sins, but physicians long perceived them as symptoms of mental disease. Among medieval scholastics, the sin *acedia* became integrated into theories of the passions, moving it nearer medical thought. Although from its earliest beginnings *acedia* contained the sense of *tristitia*, dejection about worldly matters, from the time of Cassian until the early Middle Ages *acedia* was primarily associated with the troubles that beset religious contemplatives. For St. Thomas Aquinas (1225?–1274), who thought it a kind of *tristitia*, *acedia* became manifest when the concupiscible desires caused the will to become diverted from moving toward some good. Eventually the idea of *acedia* was absorbed into medical thinking on melancholy, which included boredom and self-loathing. In *The Parson's Tale*, for example, Chaucer could be drawing on either medieval religious or scientific thinking when he writes, "envye and ire maken bitterness in herte; which bitterness is moder of Accidie" (cited by Altschule, 119). Stanley Jackson comments, in *Melancholia and Depression*, on the relationship between the medieval view of the sin and the disease, melancholy, "The symptoms of this condition were intimately associated with the struggles of the anchorites against the hazards of isolation and the temptations of their own fleshly inclinations while they strove for spiritual perfection and oneness with God" (65). William Langland's portrait of Sloth the Parson in the B-text of *Piers Plowman* verges on a caricature: a member of the clergy who has waged a decidedly losing battle for some 30 years confesses that he cannot remember his *paternoster*, but knows well secular literature such as the rhymes of Robyn Hood and Randolf Earl of Chester; he is always preoccupied with tavern gossip, but cannot concentrate on God's Passion; he never visits the feeble or the incarcerated; and he would rather lead a sporting life than read the gospels (*Passus V,* 392–422). Though during the Middle Ages melancholy was mainly regarded as a mental disease and treated by the church writers as related to *acedia* (which had always been linked to sin and sadness), the Aristotelian view of melancholy as an aspect of great talent in the arts and sciences was never completely lost.

In Marsilio Ficino's *De Vita Triplici* (1482–89), there is a reassessment of the Aristotelian position on the problem of creativity. He brought Aristotle and Plato together by concluding that only those who had the saturnine temperament were capable of Plato's divine madness. Thereafter, even moderately talented men were considered melancholic, and major artistic achievement, thought dependent on the author's having been born under the planet Saturn. Given the Aristotelian-Ficinian position on melancholy as the temperament of the contemplative artist, it is reasonable to suppose that poets and physicians, as men of talent in the fields of arts and science, will not only have much to say about melancholy but will say many of the same things in the language of their separate disciplines. Certainly in the medieval and Renaissance medical treatises there is a remarkable continuity in writings about melancholy.

Views of Melancholy in Antiquity

Born of Greek parents in Pergamon in A.D. 129, the celebrated physician Galen received most of his medical education in Alexandria. His learning was based on the writings of Hippocrates, Aristotle and the physicians writing in the 500-year period following the death of Hippocrates (their works are not extant). Some of Galen's writings were studied during the Middle Ages. His treatise, *On the Affected Parts (De locis affectis),* was composed after A.D. 192 and book 3 of the work discusses the brain and spinal cord. According to J. C. Ackermann, this treatise was translated into Arabic and Hebrew, and Avicenna wrote commentaries on it.[6]

Galen believed that the brain, not the heart—as Aristotle had said—was the center of the nervous system. His discussion of the brain and spinal cord in *On the Affected Parts* contains his observations on melancholia. He believed it occurred "when black bile overflows into the substance of the brain itself... and provokes violent delirium in the presence or absence of fever, because it occupies the substance of the brain itself" (3.9.88). This humour, Galen believed, tended to be produced by "lean persons with a darker complexion, much hair and large veins" (3.10.90). His overall description of melancholic patients suggests a background of careful clinical observation:

> Fear generally befalls the melancholic patients, but the same type of abnormal sensory images *(phantasion)* do not always present themselves. As for instance, one patient believes that he has been turned into a kind of snail and therefore runs away from everyone he meets lest [its shell] should get crushed; or when another patient sees some crowing cocks flapping their wings to their song, he beats his own arms against his ribs and imitates the voice of the animals. Again, another patient is afraid that Atlas who supports the world will become tired and throw it away and he and all of us will be crushed and pushed together. And there are a thousand other imaginary ideas.
>
> Although each melancholic patient acts quite differently than the others, all of them exhibit fear or despondency. They find fault with life and hate people; but not all want to die. For some the fear of death is of principal concern during melancholy. Others again will appear to you quite bizarre because they dread death and desire to die at the same time.
>
> Therefore, it seems correct that *Hippocrates* classified all their symptoms into two groups: fear and despondency. (3.10.93)

Galen's treatment was based upon the humoural pathology

of classical Greece and Rome, and therefore he advises physicians to aim, above all things, at preserving a balance between the opposite qualities of moist and dry. In cases where the patient's entire body was found to contain atrabilious or "melancholy blood," he recommended phlebotomy, as much as the patient's body would permit, but when madness arose only from disease of the brain, bloodletting was to be avoided. Galen also gives a long list of foods producing melancholy—notably, the meat of goats, oxen, bulls, asses, camels, foxes, dogs, hares, wolves and boars. Among creatures of the sea producing atrabilious blood he named snails, tuna fish, whale, seal, dolphins and dog sharks. Among plants, he mentions only the cabbage. Especially to be avoided was thick, dark wine. For Galen, melancholy was a condition caused by thickened blood; it produced black bile, which, exhaled into the brain, caused melancholy symptoms to affect the mind.

By the second half of the ninth century, nearly all Galen's works had been translated into Arabic. "It could not be otherwise," as Manfred Ullmann observes, "for, since the third century, Galen's medicine had been completely dominant in the east of the Hellenistic world" (10). The work of Hippocrates was nearly as well known in the Arabic world—indeed, Arab doctors took the Hippocratic oath—but fewer of Hippocrates's works were translated.

Views of Melancholy in the Middle Ages

The thinking of Hippocrates and Galen survived in commentaries written in antiquity by the Byzantine compilers, notably Paul of Aegina (625–690), who probably experienced Alexandria's fall into the hands of the Arabs in 642. Through these writers, the Greek medical tradition entered the Arabic world and eventually was translated into Latin in the later Middle Ages. Paul takes up the subject of melancholy in book 3, section 14 of his

Epitome Medica, wherein he defines the disease as "a disorder of the intellect without fever, occasioned mostly by a melancholic humour seizing the understanding; sometimes the brain being primarily affected, and sometimes it being altered by sympathy with the rest of the body" (in *The Seven Books of Paulus Aegineta,* I, 383).[7] He included among the symptoms of melancholy fear, despondency and misanthropy. Melancholics, he found, sometimes imagined themselves to be brute animals and imitated their cries; sometimes they believed themselves to be earthen vessels and feared being broken. Others desired death, while still others feared dying. Some laughed incessantly, some cried.

Paul of Aegina's recommended cure for those whose melancholy was "from a primary affection of the brain" included frequent baths, a humid diet and "exhilaration of mind."[8] His treatment coincides with that of Galen, which also aimed to cure melancholia in its early stages with baths and a moist diet. Failing with these simple means, Paul recommended stronger measures: the drinking of acrid vinegar, presumably to thin thick humours, and, if need be, phlebotomy. When the patient's strength returned after phlebotomy, Paul advised purging "downwards, with wild cucumber, and the composition from the black hellebore" to "promote the hemorrhoidal and menstrual discharges, if the affection be occasioned by retention of them" (*The Seven Books of Paulus Aegineta* I, 384).[9]

The writings of Paul of Aegina, along with the treatises of Alexander of Tralles (525–605) and Oribasius of Pergamon (325–403), are at the center of that Byzantine medicine that conveyed the Greek medical tradition—in essence, the learning of Galen and Hippocrates—to the East via Arabic (in the form of encyclopedias and other compilations suitable for use as textbooks) and to the West via Latin. Oribasius's description of sadness and fear as primary symptoms of melancholy and his prescribed treatments are all familiar derivatives of observations in Galen's *De Melancholia,* possibly a work recorded by a sixth century Byzantine author, Aetius of Amida, who was active at the time of Justinian, who reigned from 527–567. Also derived from this Galenic work is Oribasius's detailed account of a special class of melancholy, which we will return to in the chapter on Chaucer's *Book of the Duchess.* Oribasius describes the dramatic melancholy syndrome, "lycanthropy," this way:

> Those who are beset by this evil go out of their houses at night and imitate wolves in all things. Until dawn they wander among the tombs of the dead. You can know them by the following traits: they are pale, their eyes are dull, dry, tearless, and sunken. Their tongue is extremely dry; almost no saliva is seen in their mouth; they are dying of thirst; their legs are incurably wounded because they keep bumping into things at night. These are the traits of those people. What you have to know about this matter is that lycanthropy is a species of melancholy, which at the time of its onset you will be able to cure by cutting a vein and drawing blood up to the point of causing death.

After mentioning the usefulness of baths, the Byzantine compiler also discusses appropriate food and drink for the suffering patient:

> I make use of milk for three days. You will be able to purge him once, twice, and three times with the antidote of colocynth. After the purgings I give an antidote from vipers and likewise others which are recorded in the cures for melancholy. When the disease attacks the sick person is to be sprinkled with those things which ordinarily induce sleep. And when he is asleep his ears and nostrils are to be smeared with opium.[10]

Though Oribasius's discussion appears under the rubric, "Concerning Lycanthropy," his observations resemble some Arabic commentaries, as we shall see in later chapters, concerning *cotorub* or canine melancholy (*melancholia canina*), another seeming transformation of human into animal. His description of the eyes of those made melancholy by disappointment in love, found in the section "On Lovers," resembles what he says about the eyes of those suffering wolf madness: their eyes were hollow, tearless, filled with a voluptuous look, and their eyelids blinked continuously. The interesting point here is that later Arabic medical writers tend to fuse love melancholy and *melancholia canina,* or what they call *cucubut.*

Arabic medicine, as represented in the writing of such physicians as Rhazes (865–923), Haly Abbas (d. 994) and Avicenna (980–1037), develops out of the Byzantine compilers and it, too, becomes part of the literature of the Latin West, owing largely to translations of Arabic into Latin, beginning with the work of Constantine the African and Gerard of Cremona in the later Middle Ages.

Haly Abbas (Ali ibn al-Abbas) represented the state of Arabic scholarship before Avicenna and his *Liber totius medicine,* first published in 1492, was known as the "royal book." In the section of this work called *Theorice,* Haly Abbas takes up the subject of black melancholy or "natural melancholy." He tried to account for the wide variety of behavior in those who suffer from melancholia, without drawing on the possibility of the modifying effect of the other three kinds of humours:

> Black melancholy of the mind is something spread without fever; which happens either as the result of illness of the brain itself or from its connection with other members which participate in the illness. And when this happens as a result of the illness of the brain itself, it is from a build up of the humour of black bile, which is formed in the brain itself or ascends to the brain from the illness of the stomach; they collect in the brain bit by bit, and in this way become observable. When they are present the humours are burned up, but the soul becomes disturbed and thought is diminished.
>
> The following are the causes of this participation of the brain with the other members. Some of the vapors and

black humours from the humours which are burnt up there ascend from the stomach and the places under the hypochondrium to the brain; this illness is referred to as "ascending." Sometimes this happens because they ascend to the brain from all parts of the body when the humours are burned up. It does not, however, happen this way if the illness is the result of fear or sadness. And universally for all who suffer from foolishness the black signs are memory, fear, and bad judgment. Some of those to whom this happens fear death, and some long for it.

Some laugh increasingly, some cry. Some of them deny themselves and say that they do not exist. Some think that they are clay pots and beg not to be broken. Some think that they are some kind of irrational animal and cry out with animal voices.[11]

Note how Haly Abbas's writings echo the perspectives and ideas Galen voiced 800 years earlier.

The major transmitter of early Arabic medicine to the West is Constantine the African (Constantinus Africanus, A.D. 1010–1087). His chapters on melancholy found in the *Pantegni*—sometimes called *Theorica* in the literature—are his translation of Haly Abbas. Constantine translated the most important Arabic medical writings that had appeared by the mid-eleventh century. Legend has it that after years of traveling in the East, he became a member of the Benedictine community of Monte Cassino, where he spent the last 15 years of his life translating as many as 40 Greco-Arabic works from Arabic into Latin. His *De Melancholia*, long attributed to Constantine himself, is now commonly considered a translation from an Arabic writer, probably Ishaq ibn Imran.[12] There are two observations worth making about this subtle work. First, in translating it, Constantine, like both Haly Abbas and Avicenna, draws attention to the variety, even contradictory features of melancholy:

Some . . . like solitude and darkness and withdrawal from society. Others like open and sunlit spaces, meadows, fruitbearing and stream-fed gardens. Others like to ride horseback, listen to a variety of music, and to converse with wise and enjoyable people. . . . Still others sleep to excess, others weep, and others laugh.[13]

Constantine also attends to the spiritual dimension of the experience of melancholy. Second, speaking of the studious, the philosophical, the scientific, he writes:

> It will be enough to talk about the bodily causes of melancholy. It is appropriate therefore, as we promised, to speak of the things that pertain to the soul. The soul acts in a changeable fashion—in wrath, in calm, etc. . . . these kinds of melancholics are comparable: they are studious in the sciences, they fatigue their memories, they grow sad from the exhaustion of their souls, and they become rigid in their principles. All these things cause their memories and reasons and intellects to fail. As Hippocrates said (*Epidemica* VI), for the soul, thought is work (as walking, which produces such awful ills, is for the body).[14]

It was Constantine's influence, however, as a translator, rather than as an author in his own right, that helped lead to the state in western medicine in which men believed "that he who would be a good doctor must be a good Avicennist" (Ullmann, 54).

The most famous of Arabic physicians and philosophers, Abu Ali Husain ibn Abdullah ibn Sina, commonly known in Latin as Avicenna, was born in Afsena in the district of Bokhara, one of the leading cultural centers of the Moslem world. Avicenna's fame as a physician rests on the *Qanun* (known in English as the *Canon*), a massive work, five books long, originally translated from Arabic into Latin by Gerard of Cremona at Toledo before 1187, and later improved by the great doctor and orientalist, Andrea Alpago (d. 1522). Constantine did not translate Avicenna's *Canon*, possibly because his fascination with Arabic medical encyclopedism was already satisfied by producing his *Pantegni* from translations of the writings of Haly Abbas. Avicenna's work gained notice in the west by the second quarter of the thirteenth century, and it rapidly won an important place in medieval western European medicine, at least in part, as Nancy Siraisi points out in her recent book, *Avicenna in Italy*, because of "the philosophical context in which Avicenna succeeded in placing medicine" (40). Avicenna's *Canon* retained its prominence as a textbook in western European universities even after the Middle Ages. Renaissance interest in Avicenna's medical writing is evidenced by the fact that the complete or partial text of his *Canon of Medicine* in Latin was printed in 60 editions between 1500 and 1674 (Siraisi, 3). The work was the most popular of all his writings, and it earned Avicenna the reputation as "prince of physicians." Dante placed him in Limbo with other noble personages who lived without Christian revelation:

> Euclid geometra e Tolomeo,
> Ipocrate, Avicenna e Galieno,
> Averois, che 'l gran comento feo.
>
> > (*Inferno* 4.142–44)[15]

He was also among the medical authorities known to Geoffrey Chaucer's Doctour of Phisik:

> Wel knew he the olde Esculapius,
> And Deyscorides, and eek Rufus,
> Olde Ypocras, Haly, and Galyen,
> Serapion, Razis, and Avycen,
> Averrois, Damascien, and Constantyn,
> Bernard, and Gatesden, and Gilbertyn.[16]

Avicenna placed melancholy within the system of the four humours; his view is ultimately derived from Galen:

> Unnatural melancholy.... is like something burned down to ashes.... But melancholy that is overflowing is another one that is ashes of bile and its conflagration. And it is bitter; between it and red bile that we recognize to have been burned, there is this difference, that it is red bile into which these ashes have been mixed. But this

adds up to nothing but ashes separated by themselves whose thin properties have been refined. Another case is that of the ashes of phlegm and what was burned off from it. And if the phlegm was very thin and watery its ashes will be salty, and if not will be drawn to [acredinem] or [ponticitatem?]. Another kind is the ashes of blood and what is burned off from it, and this kind is sharp, and verges on a bit of sweetness. Another kind is the ashes of natural melancholy, which if it is thin will have ashes and what is burned off from it that are very sour like vinegar that has fallen on the earth and boiled up from it, and its odor is bitter enough to make flies flee from it. Another variety, if it is gross, will be of less pungency with [ponticitate] and bitterness. The three varieties of bad black bile, therefore, are: red bile when it is burned and its thin properties refined, and the two other kinds that we talked of after it. But phlegmatic melancholy is slower to do harm and of less intrinsic badness. It is choleric melancholy that is worse and speedier in causing corruption. But it is more susceptible of a cure than the former.[17]

Thus, apart from the natural melancholy of black bile, Avicenna assumed other types of melancholy, resulting from the other three basic humours, that could give melancholy a choleric, phlegmatic or sanguine cast. In another section of the *Canon*, Avicenna elaborates this notion of the varieties of "adust" melancholy, which came from blending black bile with blood, phlegm or yellow bile:

And we say that when black bile producing melancholy is mixed with blood, it is accompanied by joy and laughter, not intense sadness. But if it is mixed with phlegm, it is accompanied by sluggishness, shiftlessness, and quiet. And if it is mixed with bile or results from bile, it is accompanied by agitation and a kind of demonic behavior and is comparable to mania. And if the bile is pure black, then it will be accompanied by a great deal of thinking and very little agitation or disturbance unless the patient is bothered and quarrels and harbors a hatred that he has not forgotten.[18]

The medical writing on melancholia of the later Middle Ages and the Renaissance owe a great debt to the views of Avicenna, and, before him, Constantine the African and Galen, whether these authorities are referred to directly or not. Descriptions of melancholia by medical writers of the Renaissance add very little that is new to the clinical picture of the disease in the Middle Ages, but they transmitted those ideas to the learned and the laymen around them.

Views of Melancholy in the Renaissance

Sir Thomas Elyot's *The Castell of Health* (1534) is the work of a layperson who not only dared to write a medical book, but wrote it in the vernacular. This compendium of what the common person thought about medical knowledge in the sixteenth century gives some space to melancholy, offering a fair summary of ideas familiar from Galenic humoral theory. He begins his discussion with a clear description that includes a list of visible symptoms of the disease:

> Melancholike is colde and drie, ouer whome the earth hath dominion, and is perceiued by these signes following,
>> Leannes with hardnes of skinne.
>> Haire plaine and thin.
>> Colour dusketh, or white with leannes.
>> Much watch.
>> Dreames fearfull.
>> Stiffe in opinions.
>> Digestion slow and ill.
>> Timorous and fearfull.
>> Anger long fretting.
>> Pulse little.
>> Seldome laughing.
>> Urine waterie and thin. (4–5)

Elyot, repeating an idea familiar in classical and medieval writing, speaks of two kinds of melancholy, natural and unnatural. Natural melancholy, he says, "is the dregges of pure bloud, and is knowne by the blacknes when it issueth either downward or upward, and is verily cold or drie" (14). In contrast, there is unnatural melancholy, of which he writes, "[it] proceedeth of the adustion of cholerike mixture, and is hoter and lighter, hauling in it violence to kill, with a dangerous disposition" (14). When Elyot writes that melancholics suffer "fearefull dreames of terrible visions, dreaming of darknesse, deepe pittes, death of friends, or acquaintance, and of all things that is blacke" (111), he suggests the character of Hamlet who, by nature sanguine, reacts so deeply to external events that he becomes as melancholic as those diseased by imaginations affected by innate physiology. Chapters 4 and 5 on Shakespeare will return to Elyot.

He is very detailed about matters of diet affecting melancholy, and one of the most important factors to be considered about "meate and drinke" is what he calls substance—"some is good, which maketh good iuyce and good bloud: some is ill, and ingendreth ill iuyce and ill bloud" (19). Since melancholy was cold and dry, foods classified as warm and moist were, generally speaking, thought to alleviate melancholy because of their contrasting relationship to the disease. Among Elyot's recommendations for meats and drinke that make "good juice" are:

> Milke new milked dronke fasting, wherein is sugar
>   or the leaues of mints.
> Fishe of stony riuers, Veale sucking.
> Porke young, Beefe not passing three yeares old.
> Lettice, cicorie, grapes.
> Wines good moderately taken, well fined.
> Ale and Beere sixe dayes olde, cleane brewed and
>   not strong. (19)

Our ancestors knew little about diet, overate (as we do), and often had unwholesome, inadequate food. Much that went wrong with the body—including brains and nervous systems—must have been related to nutrition; any attention given to diet, therefore, may indeed be considered forward-looking and, in some measure, original.

Another important source of Renaissance thinking on melancholia is *A Treatise of Melancholie* (1586), a work which gives more attention than Elyot's to the moral dimension of the disease. Written by Timothy Bright (1550?–1615), a physician who later became a clergyman, this treatise will concern us again in the chapter on Shakespeare's *Hamlet*. From the outset, Bright makes clear in an epistle that the treatise is both a medical and theological work, for he plans to demonstrate "what the difference is betwixt natural melancholy and that heavie hand of God upon the afflicted conscience, tormented with the remorse of sinne, and fear of his judgement" (Epistle, 3). As a physician, five years away from becoming a rector in Yorkshire at the time of the treatise's publication, Bright attempted to go beyond the materialism of Galen, who saw the disease of melancholy as the consequence of the sickness of the body affecting the soul, driving it into sadness, or even insanity. Bright's treatise, like almost all studies of melancholy in the sixteenth century, is based on sound Galenism, but it makes room for such matters as stings of conscience and the ways in which "the bodie and corporall things Affect the soule, & how the body is affected of it again" (Epistle, 3). There may be in Bright something like a Protestant permutation of *acedia*, the melancholy long associated with those in the religious life. Bright must have had enormous faith in his powers as a physician, for he states his belief that "scarce appeareth any calamity, but if time be taken and opportunitie laid holde on helpe and release doth as readily present itselfe, to the comforte of such as trauaile" (Epistle, 5).

If there is an innovator in Renaissance medical thinking about melancholia, that would be Theophrastus von Hohenheim, commonly known as Paracelsus. Though Paracelsus's work on melancholy was not published until 1567, he composed it in the 1520s, shortly before the appearance of Sir Thomas Elyot's *Castell of Health*. He inherited and, to some extent, espoused views that could be called Galenic, but he added a striking new emphasis on "chemotherapy," and for that reason was largely resisted by the whole Galenic establishment. What made Paracelsus's reputation in the second half of the sixteenth and throughout the seventeenth century was his chemistry. As municipal physician in Basle, he was in a position to disseminate his views, as that position included a professorship at the university where, for a brief time, he taught medicine.

His discussion of melancholy appears in a treatise entitled, *The Diseases that Deprive Man of His Reason, Such as St. Vitus' Dance, Falling Sickness, Melancholy, and Insanity, and Their Correct Treatment*, written when Paracelsus was 30 (*Four Treatises of Theophrastus von Hohenheim*, 127–212). Most of what he has to say concerns his manner of treatment, but he does briefly define the disease and includes, as an elaboration of that definition, his understanding of the four kinds of melancholy. He considered melancholics to be insane people "who are disturbed by their own nature—there is no apparent defect of reason; their complexes are affected and they suppress reason, ruling it as they wish" (*Four Treatises*, 179). Later, it becomes clear that what he means by "their complexes" are the four humours which, according to Galen, determined temperament. Near the conclusion Paracelsus takes up the question of the "four kinds of melancholy" and explains their origin "from the four complexions":

> ... two complexions are alike: *sanguis* and *cholera* are accompanied by joy, although they are different; for one is warlike, the other is not.... The other two complexions, phlegm and melancholy, behave in the same way.... (180)

Paracelsus's distinctive contribution to evolving medical thinking on the subject of melancholy concerns his

elaboration of treatment by "opposites," a treatment specifically chemical:

> If the melancholic patient is despondent, make him well
> again by a gay medicine. If he laughs too much, make
> him well by a sad medicine. There are some medicines
> which make people laugh and make their minds happy,
> removing all diseases which have their origin in sadness:
> the entire sadness is removed. There are also medicines
> which induce sadness, in such a way that they soothe
> unseemly laughter and exaggerated, unsuitable pleasure
> by changing it. (179)

He also gives a list of particular medicines, which he
says, on the one hand, "expel all sadness," and, on the
other hand, "cause insane patients who show excessive
pleasure and voluptuousness to be naturally sad": *aurum
potabile, croci magisterium, arbor maris, ambra acuata,
letitia veneris* (180).

The *Treatise of Melancholie* written by Bright, the
physician turned clergyman, implies an optimism regarding the possibility for curing melancholy, which was
shared by other Renaissance writers. One of the famous
sixteenth century descriptions of the melancholy man
appears in André Du Lauren's *Melancholie Diseases and
... the Meanes to Cure Them* (1599), a work that, it
seems to me, had a demonstrable influence on *Hamlet*.
Because we shall return to this treatise more fully later, I
cite just a brief section of his lengthy sketch of the melancholic:

> he would runne away and cannot goe, he goeth alwaies
> sighing, troubled with the hicket, and with an vnsepar-
> able sadnes, which oftentimes turneth into dispayre. (Du
> Laurens, 82)

He concludes, nonetheless, that these "naturall inclinations ... may bee reclaimed and amended, by the qualities which we get vnto our selues by morell Philosophie,
by the reading of good bookes, and by frequenting the

companies of honest and vertuous men" (83–84). Such confidence in the possibility of achieving a cure, even a self-cure, doubtless owes something to the humanistic spirit, curious about all the capabilities of the individual, that was abroad in the Age of Elizabeth I (1558–1603). Christopher Marlowe's conquering Scythian hero, Tamburlaine the Great, expresses it this way:

> Nature that fram'd us of foure Elements,
> Warring within our breasts for regiment,
> Doth teach us all to have aspyring minds:
> Our soules, whose faculties can comprehend
> That wondrous Architecture of the world:
> And measure every wandering planets course:
> Still climbing after knowledge infinite,
> And alwaies mooving as the restles Spheares,
> Wils us to weare our selves and never rest,
> Untill we reach the ripest fruit of all.
> *(Works* I, 105; *Tamburlaine,* Pt. I, 2.7.8–27)

At roughly the same time, Sir Francis Bacon wrote to an uncle saying he had taken all knowledge as his province, and Hamlet, in the great soliloquy from act 2, exclaims, "What a piece of work is a man! How noble in reason! How infinite in faculty!" Such literary expressions of confidence in the nobility of the human spirit share place with the optimism of medical writers like Bright and Du Laurens. Several passages in *Melancholy Diseases* offer parallels to these literary statements of the Elizabethan Age's spirit of curiosity. At this point, however, let me excerpt one brief passage from chapter 1 of the Du Laurens treatise:

> The Arabians haue so highly commended it, that they haue verely beleeued, that the minde by vertue of the imagination could worke miracles, pearce the heauens, commaunde the elements, lay plaine the huge mountaines, and make mountaines of the plaine ground. . . . (76)

Such early thinking about melancholy formed part of the intellectual inheritance of both Chaucer and Shakespeare.

THE MEDICAL KNOWLEDGE OF CHAUCER AND SHAKESPEARE

Chaucer's writing indicates considerable medical knowledge, the kind one would expect to find in a university-educated physician like the Doctor of Physic described by the pilgrim Chaucer in *The Canterbury Tales*—"In al this world ne was ther noon hym lik,/To speke of phisik and of surgerye" (*General Prologue*, 412–13)—as well as the humbler kind of knowledge exemplified in a popular work like Chaucer's own *Treatise on the Astrolabe*, written to make the use of the astronomical instrument understandable to young Lewis. In this treatise, speaking in his own voice, Chaucer makes clear, that like any other citizen of the medieval world, he believed the complete practitioner had to know astronomy: "And everich of these 12 signes [of the zodiac] hath respect to a certeyn parcel of the body of a man, and hath it in governaunce; as Aries hath thin heved, and Taurus thy nekke and thy throte, Gemini thin armholes and thin armes and so furth . . ." (pp. 668–69). Contemporary treatises on popular medicine contain many such passages, and Chaucer doubtless had read some of them. There is, to cite one example, in the fourteenth century medical treatise, *The Wyse Boke of Peers of Salerne*, a passage similar to Chaucer's:

> The *propyrteys* of the planetys be almagest in the Centologye of Tholomye. Evyry lymme of many*es* bodye is rewlyd by a certeyn sygne of the zodyak wherfor*e* as seyth tholomye if ȝe be seke in any lyme Do no medycyn to the seke whan ye mone is in the sygne of the leone for it schal rather hyndyr than forther and namly fle blode letyng in the lymme at thoo tymes. As whan ares reygnyth in the hede he reygnyth holly in yat place. Taurus in the nekke *and* in the throte. Gem*in*i in ye schuldrys.[19]

The physician Chaucer describes in the *General Prologue* is a doctor of medicine who would have spent 17 years of study and teaching before beginning private practice

(Ussery, 9). The only other pilgrim traveling to Canterbury who had so much university education is the Clerk. There were very few university-trained doctors in Chaucer's day. Most of the sick in the late fourteenth and early fifteenth centuries did not have the good fortune to be treated by someone like Chaucer's physician. Patients were usually treated by barber-surgeons, who performed such operations as bleeding, tooth drawing and cauterization; midwives; apothecaries; and members of the clergy, who were long in the habit of curing men's bodies together with their souls. Except for the clergy, these other leeches were usually unlatined and, therefore, unversed in the Latin medical authorities which formed the basis of university medical training. Chaucer's physician was familiar with the authorities that university-educated physicians of his day were studying in the medical schools of Salerno, Padua, Montpellier and Paris and which could be found in monastic libraries and, it should be added, the private libraries of nobles, to which a man of Chaucer's importance would certainly have gained access. There is possibly a hint of irony about Chaucer's list of medical authorities in that it begins with "the olde Esculapius," the physician of legend whose works do not exist. In this one instance, it would seem that Chaucer's physician could only have known the name, but not the body of work. However, since many medical works were wrongly attributed to the legendary founder of medicine during the Middle Ages, among them an abridgement of the works of Caelius Aurelianus (see p. 44), these may be the ones the physician really knew. The doctor's private arrangements with apothecaries, which contribute to their mutual profits, his love of gold and the fine clothes and food it can buy, all reflect on his moral character, but they do not detract from his skill as a physician.

Chaucer leaves no doubt that his Doctor is the thing itself: his 44-line description presents the kind of contemporary physician who truly was "a verray, parfit praktisour." Chaucer wants us to perceive him as one of that small, elite group of university-trained physicians of the day. The 15 authorities we are told the Doctor of Physic "Wel knew" (*Gen. Prol.*, 429–34) were among those that any graduate physician would have cited with confidence during the fourteenth century. If that other well-trained professional among Chaucer's pilgrims, the Man of Law, fell ill, he would have wanted to be healed by someone like his fellow traveler. Along with the doctor's familiarity with the medical authorities, he had considerable erudition in astronomy. Medieval physicians frequently carried with them a small handbook known as a *vade mecum*, which typically contained a calendar, canons of the eclipses of the sun, canons of the eclipses of the moon, tables of the planets and other information considered necessary to the correct diagnosis and treatment of disease in the Middle Ages. When Chaucer elaborates on the physicians's knowledge of astronomy and refers to the hot, cold, moist and dry humours in the blood, he is not describing a charlatan but a man who, for his day, had what it took:

> He kepte his pacient a ful greet deel
> In houres by his magyk natureel.
> Wel koude he fortunen the ascendent
> Of his ymages for his pacient.
> He knew the cause of everich maladye,
> Were it of hoot, or coold, or moyste or drye,
> And where they engendred, and of what humour.
>
> (415–21)

Galen's theory of the humours and astrology held their ground in medicine well into the fifteenth, sixteenth and early seventeenth centuries.

However, as with many accepted medical practices of today, the theories of the humours and of astrology could be used by detractors. What Chaucer presents as evidence of professional competence, other medieval writers use for attack. In another contemporary text, *Renart le*

Contrefait, as Jill Mann indicates, when Renart the Fox becomes a doctor, he is concerned with two things: knowing the correct medical authorities,

> alleguoie Galien
> Et si monstroie oeuvre ancienne
> Et de Rasis et d'Avicenne. . . . [20]

and being able to display knowledge of astronomy,

> Et avec le phiscien
> Faisoie l'astromien.
> Je nommoie signes et poins
> Et des constellacions les poins,
> Les planettes et les figures.[21]

In the medieval French work, medical authorities and the physician's use of astronomy are made materials for attack; Chaucer reserves satire for the personal side of his doctor's life. In any case, evidence that medical theories can be used for different purposes by different writers does not invalidate Chaucer's extensive medical knowledge.

Shakespeare's interest in medicine, which spanned his entire career, appeared in his plays, early and late. These often demonstrate the same humoural theory as Chaucer. When Romeo abandons his futile love for Rosaline in *Romeo and Juliet*, the symptoms of love melancholy disappear and he reverts to his accustomed sanguine temperament; in *The Taming of the Shrew*, Petruchio's rough treatment "cures" Kate of her antisocial choleric disposition; a suddenly senile king in *Lear* moves from a choleric to a melancholic temperament; the hero in *Timon of Athens*, by nature sanguine, reacts to misfortune with a melancholy so profound it ends in suicide; and Antonio of *The Merchant of Venice* is chronically depressed, knowing not why he is "so sad."

The Galenic theory of the humours, however, asserting that disease arose from an imbalance in the humours of the body, was on its way to obsolescence even as Shakespeare employed it. The death blow was given by

William Harvey (1578–1657) and his discovery of the circulation of the blood. Harvey demonstrated the blood's central role in physiology, whereby substances could be demonstrated to act on the body after entering the blood stream by absorption. His scientific breakthrough was not published, however, until 1628, and Shakespeare died in 1616. There is, nonetheless, evidence in Shakespeare's writing that he understood the more modern view of human physiology. Take, for example, the description of the action of poison working through the blood in *Hamlet*.[22] "Thy uncle stole," the ghost of Hamlet's father explains to the Prince,

> With juice of cursed hebona in a vial,
> And in the porches of my ears did pour
> The leprous distillment, *whose effect*
> *Holds such an enmity with blood of man*
> *That swift as quicksilver it courses through*
> *The natural gates and alleys of the body*
> (emphasis mine; 1.5.61–67)

Shakespeare's sense of the movement of blood through the veins as the conveyer of poison to various parts of the body is also evident in Romeo's brief remark to the Mantuan apothecary,

> let me have
> A dram of poison, such soon-speeding gear
> As will disperse itself through all the veins.
> (*Romeo and Juliet* 5.1.59–61)

Yet another example, suggesting Shakespeare's advanced sense of physiology, is Falstaff's comment on sherry in the bloodstream,

> The second property of your excellent sherris is
> the warming of the blood, which before (cold
> and settled) left the liver white and pale, which
> is the badge of pusillanimity and cowardice; but
> the sherris warms it, and *makes it course from*
> *the inwards to the parts extremes.*
> (emphasis mine; *Henry IV, Part II*; 4.3.102–07)

Despite the late publication, in 1628, of Harvey's views, *Exercitatio anatomica de motu cordis et sanguinis*, it appears they had gained some currency in London before that date.

Like Shakespeare, Harvey lived in London and enjoyed the favor of the throne. In 1604, a young doctor of medicine from Padua, back in London for two years, William Harvey married the daughter of Dr. Lancelot Browne, former physician to Queen Elizabeth I. By June 1607 Harvey became a fellow of the Royal College of Physicians, and King James I himself supported his application for the position of Physician to St. Bartholomew's hospital. In 1616 he was presenting his views on the action of the blood and heart in a formal series of lectures at the Royal College of Physicians, and he numbered among his patients such men as Lord Arundel, Francis Bacon and the king. Evidently not a man to take reckless chances, Harvey did not publish his theory until he had been lecturing on his ideas for more than 12 years; by then he had gradually demonstrated his theory of the circulation to both students and colleagues at the medical college. Thus, by publication time, Harvey's views on the circulation of the blood must already have been familiar to many Londoners. And even before he gave his first formal lectures at the College of Physicians, 24-year-old William Harvey, doctor of medicine, must have headed home to London from Padua in 1602 eager to discuss new ideas sparked by Fabricius's anatomy lectures.

Shakespeare-as-physiologist may seem ahead of his time, but the real wonder is Shakespeare the psychologist. Well before the publication of Burton's *Anatomy of Melancholy*, Shakespeare's plays reveal a profound understanding of the subject. Burton's vast encyclopedic account would not only synthesize major classical, medieval and Renaissance writing on the subject of melancholy, but formulate a succinct definition that still holds up—"Fear and Sorrow are the true characters, and inseparable companions, of most melancholy." This definition pinpoints what in melancholy makes it a congenial subject for poetry: to feel fear and sorrow is to be human, and no poet has understood more or told us better what it is to be human. Shakespeare has even told us indirectly through one of his characters that he understood the extremes of sorrow and fear that went with the disease we now recognize as schizophrenia. The words the poet gives Edgar, as he plans to imitate Poor Tom the Bedlamite, depict what Shakespeare probably took as his model:

> My face I'll grime with filth,
> Blanket my loins, elf all my hair in knots,
> And with presented nakedness outface
> The winds and persecutions of the sky.
> *The country gives me proof and president*
> *Of Bedlam beggars, who, with roaring voices,*
> *Strike in their numb'd and mortified arms*
> *Pins, wooden pricks, nails*
> (emphasis mine; *King Lear* 2.3.9–16)

There is, of course, a great difference between Edgar's description, suggesting the last stages of schizophrenia, and the kinds of behavior induced by delusions, based on fear, known to accompany severe melancholy. Consider one instance cited in the notes of Richard Napier, a physician and clergyman whose medical records, kept from 1597–1634, are the source of Michael McDonald's study of madness in seventeenth century England. "Extreme melancholy," Napier writes,

> possessing her for a longtime, with fear; and sorely tempted not to touch anything for fear that then she shall be tempted to wash her clothes, even upon her back. Is tortured until that she be forced to wash her clothes, be them never so good and new. Will not suffer her husband, child, nor any of the household to have any new clothes until they wash them for fear the dust of them will fall upon her. Dareth not to go to the church for treading on the ground, fearing lest any dust should fall upon them. (MacDonald, 154)

Alice Davy's melancholy fear of dirt is not unlike the obsessive concern with her hands Shakespeare invented for Lady Macbeth: "It is an accustom'd action with her, to seem thus washing her hands. I have known her continue in this a quarter of an hour" (*Macbeth* 5.1.28–30).

Moderate forms of melancholy, however, conferred a kind of distinction, so that the disease won favor with the genteel and learned. Citing numerous letters written to Napier by the aristocrats and gentry among his patients, McDonald observes that "Persons of rank and learning frequently judged themselves to be melancholy rather than merely sad, troubled, or fearful" (152). They seemed to be not only well-informed, perhaps as a consequence of the educated elite's interest in classical learning, but in good company as well. According to Napier's notes on his melancholy patients "40% of them were peers, knights and ladies, or masters and mistresses" (MacDonald, 151). The Aristotelian association of melancholy and creativity, learning, even genius, also lent status to its milder forms. The idea of meditative, "good" melancholy is affirmed in Milton's *Il Penseroso*:

> And may at last my weary age
> Find out the peaceful hermitage,
> The Hairy Gown and Mossy Cell,
> Where I may sit and rightly spell
> Of every star that Heav'n doth shew,
> And every Herb that sips the dew;
> Till old experience do attain
> To something like Prophetic strain;
> These pleasures *Melancholy* give,
> And I with thee will choose to live.
>
> (*Complete Poems*, 76)

Perhaps more remarkable, as portraiture of melancholy goes, is the account of the feeling of sadness with which Antonio opens Shakespeare's *The Merchant of Venice*:

> In sooth, I know not why I am so sad;
> It wearies me, you say it wearies you;

But how I caught it, found it, or came by it,
What stuff 'tis made of, whereof it is born,
I am to learn;
and such a want-wit sadness makes of me,
That I have much ado to know myself.

(1.1.1–7)

This comes close to what a good listener, like Richard Napier, might have repeated to a fellow astrologer about one of his bewildered, bored patients who was struggling to comprehend a sense of sadness without cause. Shakespeare's quickly sketched character, the merchant's friend who "knows" what makes businessmen depressed, offers one possibility:

Believe me, sir, had I such venture forth,
The better part of my affections would
Be with my hopes abroad. . . .
And every object that might make me fear
Misfortune to my ventures, out of doubt
Would make me sad.

(1.1.15–22)

The pragmatic business motive for melancholy might do for one such as Salanio, but Shakespeare has shown us with that bold introduction to Antonio's character, with which the play begins, that Salanio's evaluation is insufficient to explain his friend. To Salanio's suggestion that business ventures have made him gloomy, Antonio responds that such is not the cause. Likewise, when love is put forward as a possibility, Antonio simply utters, "Fie, fie!" (1.1.47).

Another of Shakespeare's characters puzzled by his own sense of sadness is the otherwise forgettable villain of *Much Ado about Nothing*, the bastard, Don John:

I cannot hide what I am: I must be sad when I
have cause, and smile at no man's jests; eat when
I have stomach, and wait for no man's leisure;
sleep when I am drowsy, and tend to no man's

business; laugh when I am merry, and claw no man
in his humor.

(1.3.13–18)

The "cause" of his sadness seems related to his jealousy
of Claudio, who has won favors from John's legitimate
brother: "That young start-up hath all the glory of my
overthrow./If I can cross him any way,/I bless myself
every way." (1.3.66–68). Earlier Don John suggests that
the relationship between this external cause and its
effect on feeling conspire to make his sadness no less profound than Antonio's: "There is no measure in the occasion that breeds,/Therefore the sadness is without limit"
(1.3.3–4). Don John's sense of limitless sadness suggests
an infinity of pain that makes the anxiety about measur-
ing time in the sonnets and *Troilus and Cressida* seem
self-indulgent by contrast.

Shakespeare was also interested in levels of sorrow so
great as to lead to delusions. In one of Macbeth's, the
sense of hearing is affected:

Methought I heard a voice cry "Sleep no more!
Macbeth does murther sleep"—the innocent sleep,
Sleep that knits up the ravell'd sleave of care,
The death of each day's life, sore labor's bath,
Balm of hurt minds, great nature's second course,
Chief nourisher in life's feast.

(*Macbeth* 2.2.32–37)

Macbeth's long dwelling upon the accomplishment of
Duncan's murder and the consequences of regicide
brought him to the peak of mental agitation. Once the
murder was undertaken, the burden of guilt, added to
protracted mental excitement, lead to hallucination.
This is precisely the kind of situation Michel Foucault
has in mind when, in a discussion of passion and delirium, he observes of the ancient Romans that the life of
the city and the court could lead to madness by a "multi-
plicity of excitations constantly accumulated, prolonged,
and echoed" which, allowed to escalate to a certain

point, "can lead to delirium" (90–91). The voice Macbeth imagines in this passage makes concrete his sense of emotional disarray by announcing he can no longer be at rest—"Sleep no more!" The voice's announcement, moreover, that "Macbeth does murther sleep," in reminding us that Duncan was asleep when Macbeth went to kill him, implies an identity between the peace of sleep and the innocent, good king. Macbeth has destroyed the peace of order embodied in the king, and his crimes deprive him of that "balm of hurt minds."

The significance of sleep and sleeplessness in melancholia will be explored further in the following chapter on Chaucer's *Book of the Duchess*, the poet's first important long narrative poem. In it he displays a subtle understanding of complex mental states that goes beyond what we generally mean when we use such terms as "received knowledge" or "popular culture."

Two

The Book of the Duchess

Chaucer and the Medieval Physicians

C omparing Chaucer's understanding of mental states, as it appears in *The Book of the Duchess*, with those ideas recorded in medical texts makes even more evident the human values in the poem to which generations of readers have responded. Examining Chaucer thus is not an unliterary approach. Even Robert Jordan, examining the poem to uncover the general principles that preside over its status as literary discourse, gets dangerously close to meaning (for a critical theorist) when he points to the fact that 1,000 lines of this 1,300-line poem are elegiac (60). It has been called "the most historically contextualized of Chaucer's early narrative poems" (Edwards, 64). Chaucer himself makes the poem part of the history of his time by tying it to the death of John of Gaunt's wife, Blanche; he has Queen Alceste, in *The Legend of Good Women*, refer to the poem as "the Deeth of Blaunche the Duchesse" (418). As this historical reference dictates the gravity of the poem's opening, so its other historical components sharpen and season its tone. Medical knowledge is one of those components.

The varying ways in which Chaucer's *Book of the Duchess* portrays and addresses melancholy deserve a more comprehensive examination, particularly in terms of what medical texts reveal. Descriptions of three diseases are almost always found in close proximity to one another in early medical treatises: melancholy, *hereos* and mania. Distinguishing between them is complicated by the fact that these diseases had a number of symptoms in common. It is not surprising, therefore, to find that Stanley Jackson begins his study, *Melancholia and Depression*, with these words:

> In the terms *melancholia* and *depression* and their cognates, we have well over two millennia of the Western world's ways of referring to a goodly number of different dejected states. At any particular time during these many centuries the term that was in common use might have denoted a disease, a troublesome condition of sufficient severity and duration to be conceived of as a clinical entity; or it might have referred to one of a cluster of symptoms that were thought to constitute a disease. (3)

But as a point from which to begin, it is probably safe to generalize by saying that medieval physicians meant by *depression* or *melancholia* a disease in which sadness and fear were dominant emotions and the imagination disordered, by *mania* a disease in which the prime emotion was anger with some disturbance of the imagination and, to a lesser degree, reason, and by *hereos*—a disease that always ended in mania—a type of melancholia characterized by an obsessive preoccupation with a beloved person. While these definitions are basic, one always has to be prepared for slight variations as, for example, in these definitions of melancholy and mania derived from Constantine, included by Bartholomaeus Anglicus in his Latin encyclopedia, and retranslated into Middle English by John of Trevisa in the fourteenth century:

> As Constantinus seiþ *in libro de melancolia*, melancolia he seiþ is a *sus*[p]eccioun þat hatte *mania* and madnes þat hatte malencolia, by diuers greuynge and hurtinge of worchinge, for [in] *mania* principalich þe ymaginacioun is ihurt [and in þe oþ ir resoun is ihurt.] (I, liber 7, capitulum 6, 349–50)

Since John Livingston Lowes published his seminal article, "The Loveres Maladye of Hereos," in 1914, more and more literary scholars have been turning their attention to those hard-to-locate, mostly unpublished medical manuscripts by such early physicians as Rhazes (al-Razi), Avicenna, Arnald of Villanova, Bernard of Gordon and Valescus de Taranta—writing that earlier had been the exclusive domain of the historians of medicine.[1] Lowes, in that early effort in interdisciplinary studies, clearly demonstrated that Chaucer's description of Arcite's physical and mental condition in the *Knight's Tale* is a close parallel to passages about *hereos* found in medical treatises from ancient times through the Middle Ages and early Renaissance. Though Lowes intended to extend his study of particular literary works, in terms of the medical materials, beyond Chaucer's *Knight's Tale*, he never did. On *The Book of the Duchess*, however, he did comment that "The famous opening lines . . . read with what we know of *hereos* in mind, reflect at point after point the conventional symptoms" (543–44).

In their efforts to identify the disease the narrator of *The Book of the Duchess* has suffered for eight long years, several modern scholars have already attempted a more complete evaluation of the evidence. John Hill pointed out that "One of the most prominent symptoms of love melancholy, fixation on the object of desire is missing" (38); Judith Neaman concluded that the narrator suffers from ordinary melancholy, the main consequence of which is an inability to write (101–13); and, in a recent note, I argued that the narrator of Chaucer's poem is an example of a neglected variety of melancholy known in the medical literature as *melancholia canina* (185–90). In broader terms, John B. Friedman, in a 1969 *Chaucer Review* article, described the narrator of the poem as spiritually distressed (145–62). In discussing Chaucer's concern with poetic subjectivity, Robert Edwards, in his recent book on the dream visions, has made a telling observation, "We might take this [the account of the narrator's mental state] as the originary gesture of his narrative for he explicitly identifies the narrator's interior world as 'our first mater' (43) and 'my first matere' (218)" (68). That is, the primary subject of Chaucer's poem is the anguished inward life of the narrator, to which the outward dream bears witness.

I think on reconsidering the evidence—the poem itself and the medical treatises— that the pathological condition described in *The Book of the Duchess*, both in its symptomatology and treatment, cannot be identified as a clear-cut case of lovesickness as set forth in discussions by classical and medieval physicians. Furthermore, making clear distinctions between *amor hereos*, melancholy and mania is difficult because early descriptions of these diseases—particularly their treatments—tend to overlap. The difficulty is worth coping with, however; exploring Chaucer's poetic descriptions of melancholy and the medical discussions of the disease by classical and medieval physicians reveals the kind of striking similarities that imply close interrelationships between medieval poetry and medieval medicine. In studying the resemblances between Chaucer's poetry and medieval medical thinking on melancholy, more light can be shed on the poet's keen psychological perceptiveness, as well as on the breadth of knowledge that fed his poetic imagination. Early physicians may have diagnosed and written about mental disorders, but Chaucer's poetry contributed much to popularizing their thinking.

Part of the task of this chapter will be to examine the way sleeping, reading and talking are used by classical and medieval physicians to treat the symptoms of mental diseases and the extent to which Chaucer's suffering narrator-dreamer employs these same three "cures."

SLEEPLESSNESS

The Book of the Duchess begins with a portrait of a narrator rendered sleepless by a great sorrow; whether it be "unfulfilled desire" (Robertson and Huppé, 32) or "a general, unfathomable state of *melancholia*" (Hill, 38) is not immediately clear.

> I have gret wonder, be this lyght,
> How that I lyve, for day ne nyght
> I may nat slepe wel nygh noght;
> I have so many an ydel thoght,
> Purely for defaute of slep.
>
> (*Duchess* 1–5)

The passage, Robinson points out in the Explanatory Notes to his edition, resembles both the opening of Froissart's *Paradys d'Amours* and several passages in Machaut's *Dit de la Fonteinne Amoureuse* (773). He adds that the situation described was one which "according to medieval theory or general human experience would have led to dreams" (774). The problem of whether Chaucer or other medieval poets had direct knowledge of scientific treatises or were drawing on observable human experiences is one we will put aside for now and return to later in the chapter. Suffice to say, at this juncture, the comment is correct; a dream does occur, but not until the theme of sleep is worked through. The narrator goes on at length with a discourse about his condition in which the word "sleep" frequently appears, as, for example, in this brief excerpt:

And wel ye woot, agaynes kynde
Hyt were to lyven in thys wyse,
For nature wolde nat suffyse
To noon erthly creature
Nat longe tyme to endure
Withoute slep and be in sorwe.

(16–21)

Something is dangerously wrong; life cannot be maintained for long without sleep. In an effort to conquer his sleeplessness, the narrator turns to reading the eleventh book of Ovid's *Metamorphoses*, the story of Ceyx and Alcyone, married lovers separated by death. Suspending for now discussion of what the narrator may have gained by his emotional involvement with the grieving wife of Ovid's tale, we see immediately that the discovery of the god of sleep is crucial for him. Chaucer handles the section on the intervention of the god with a light, comic touch that throws the tragic circumstances into high relief. To answer Alcyone's prayer for information about her husband's fate, Juno sends a messenger in quest of a revelatory dream from the Cave of Sleep. The messenger can hardly rouse the god, in a passage Chaucer modulates comically without allowing the tone to become jarring:

This messager com fleynge faste
And cried, "O, ho! awake anoon!"
Hit was for noght; there herde hym non.
"Awake!" quod he, "whoo ys lyth there?"
And blew his horn ryght in here eere,
And cried "Awaketh!" wonder hye.

(178–83)

The poem continues the elaboration of the theme of sleep in the following section, in which the narrator, much struck by his reading of the account of "the goddes of slepyng" (230), prays to the newly discovered Morpheus who brought sleep to Queen Alcyone:

Me thoghte wonder yf hit were so,
For I had never herd speke, or tho

Of noo goddes that koude make
Men to slepe, ne for to wake,
For I ne knew never god but oon.
And in my game I sayde anoon
(And yet me lyst ryght evel to pleye).

(233–39)

If only Morpheus will let him "slepe a lyte" (249), the narrator will offer the comic sacrifice of a featherbed "Of down of pure dowves white" (250) and a black and gold sleeping chamber. No sooner is the promise made than he promptly falls asleep and becomes a dreamer who has "so ynly swete a sweven" (276) that no one, not even Joseph or Macrobius, could interpret his dream.

In early medical treatises, the inability to sleep is a serious symptom, and it follows naturally enough that inducing sleep is curative. One of the first medical writers to discuss mental diseases and, in particular, melancholy and mania, was Soranus of Ephesus, who studied medicine at Alexandria and practiced at Rome during the reigns of Trajan (98–117) and Hadrian (117–138). According to his editor and translator, I. E. Drabkin, "Soranus' works, in common with Hippocratic and Galenic writings, were among those most widely excerpted and translated" (Aurelianus, *On Acute Diseases*, xi). His foremost translator was the African, Caelius Aurelianus, who probably lived in the fifth century. His major contribution to communicating Greek medicine to the Middle Ages is his translation of two important works by Soranus, the *Acute Diseases* (three books) and the *Chronic Diseases* (five books). Charles Talbot, the eminent authority on medieval medicine in England, has called this translation by Caelius Aurelianus "the main link in the transmission of ancient medical thought to the Middle Ages" ("Medicine," 393). The fate of this lengthy and popular work was to undergo changes and abridgements: the portion on acute diseases appeared alone early, with the name "Aurelius" as author; the second half on chronic diseases was circulated in the seventh century under the name "Aesculapius." These two abridgements spawned many other smaller compilations, some of which were practical, others more theoretical (Talbot, 393).[2] The two treatises examine both melancholy and mania; the latter is described as "a major disease; it is chronic and consists of attacks alternating with periods of remission; it involves a state of stricture" (Aurelianus, 541).

The question of sleep is taken up only in the section of the book that considers mania. Aurelianus cites "continual sleeplessness" as one of the "observable causes" of mania (537). Among its symptoms he lists "light and short sleep," "tossing in sleep," as well as "sleep marked by great fear and turmoil" (537). He observes that "in most cases of mania, at the time of an actual attack, the eyes become bloodshot and intent. There is also continual wakefulness" (541). Here it is a symptom or effect, not a cause. The prescribed cures were physical as well as chemical. First he writes that "If the patient is wakeful, prescribe passive exercise, first in a hammock and then in a sedan chair. The rapid dripping of water may be employed to induce sleep, for under the influence of its sound patients often fall asleep" (547). Dripping water appears within the context of sleep in both the *Book of the Duchess* and the Ceyx and Alcyone myth of Ovid's *Metamorphoses:*

> ther were a fewe welles
> Came rennynge fro the clyves adoun,
> that made a dedly slepynge soun,
> And ronnen doun ryght by a cave
> That was under a rokke ygrave
> Amydde the valey, wonder depe.
> There these goddes lay and slepe,
> Morpheus and Eclympasteyr,
> That was the god of slepes heyr,
> That slep and dide noon other werk.

(*Duchess* 160–69)

> But from the bottom of the cave there flows the stream
> of Lethe, whose waves, gently murmuring over the
> gravelly bed, invite to slumber. Before the cavern's
> entrance abundant poppies bloom, and countless herbs,
> from whose juices dewy night distils sleep and spreads
> its influence over the darkened lands.
>
> (*Metamorphoses* 11.163)[3]

Ovid's passage includes not just Lethe's drowsy streams
but other allusions as well to gentle murmuring waves,
blooming poppies and numerous night-distilling herbs,
all of which make it a comprehensive poetic treatment of
Morpheus. At a later point in his discussion of mania and
ways of enabling the patient to sleep, Caelius Aurelianus
observes that some physicians take a psychopharma-
cological approach and "try to produce a deep sleep with
certain drugs, fomenting the patient with poppy and
causing stupor and drowsiness rather than natural sleep"
(555). Of the latter approach he is obviously critical, as
he adds, "in so doing, they constrict the very parts which
require relaxing measures" (555). Indeed, Aurelianus's
preferred program of treatment was "primarily concerned
with relaxing a state of stricture" (Jackson, 35).

Another commentator on melancholy and sleeplessness is the medical compiler Paul of Aegina. Francis
Adams states that "all the medical authors . . . of the dis-
tinguished Arabian period, quote his opinions in almost
every page of their works, and never fail to recognize him
as one of the most eminent of their Grecian masters"
(*The Seven Books of Paulus Aegineta*, 3, 16 [from Intro-
duction]). During the early Middle Ages, the third book
of Paul of Aegina's *Epitome Medica* was translated into
Latin.[4] Book 3, section 14, "On Melancholy, Mania, and
Demoniacs" as well as book 3, section 18, "On Love-Sick
Persons," touch on the matter of sleep. In his chapter on
melancholy, Paul cites "want of sleep" as one of the "peculiar symptoms of melancholy" (*The Seven Books*,
3.383).[5] Later, in considering the lovesick, he states that

"Such persons" are "desponding and sleepless" (3.391)[6]—a thoroughly logical outcome, given his view of this subdivision of melancholy:

> It will not be out of place here to join love to the affections of the brain, since it consists of certain cares. For care is a passion of the soul occasioned by the reason's being in a state of laborious emotion. (3.390–91)[7]

The Arabic physicians such as Rhazes, Haly Abbas and Avicenna built on the medical tradition of Byzantine compilers such as Paul of Aegina. In the tenth century compendium of medical lore, *Continens*, Rhazes, like Paul of Aegina, draws the symptom of sleeplessness from the inherited Greco-Roman medical tradition. We find, for instance, in *Tractatus* 20, chapter 1, the following:

> The Jew said that patients with *cotorub* or *hereos* walk around like dogs at night and their faces are saffron-colored from sleeplessness. . . .
>
> Alexander said that patients with *cotorub* or *hereos* walk about making gnashing sounds, wandering, and crying out all night long especially in the burying grounds of the dead right up to morning.[8]

Rather similar is Rhazes's statement on lovesickness in his other major work, the *Liber Divisionum*, entitled "De cucubut":

> It is one species [of melancholy] which happens as a result of the burning up of blood. Its signs are an extremely downcast look, unrelieved sadness and silence, and getting up at night.[9]

Furthermore, his cure is explicitly described as resembling the treatment for melancholy, and it combines the somatic and chemical approaches familiar from Caelius Aurelianus. A sleep-inducing relaxation is the aim:

> And its cure is in the cure of melancholy practiced when melancholy is found in the whole body, namely, many

applications of oil, baths, and the kind of soporific which is poured over the head, such as a brew made of lettuce seeds, stems of poppies and dried violets, and milk emulsions; foods made from milk, squash, and almond oil should be used.[10]

During the later Middle Ages, it was common to view lovesickness as a separate disease, though many physicians, like Rhazes, related it to melancholy. The fourteenth century physician, Bernard of Gordon, places the discussion of "De amore qui hereos dicitur" after the section entitled "De mania & melancholia" in his *Lilium Medicinae*.[11] Bernard's *Lilium*, completed in 1303, was a revision of a popular textbook by Gilbert the Englishman in use at the prestigious medical school of Montpellier, still fairly new then, which began as a garden and pharmaceutical school. Indeed, as George Sarton comments, Bernard probably used Gilbert's text as a medical student "in Salerno but even if he had not, he had certainly become acquainted with it when he began his own teaching in Montpellier, c. 1283" ("Lilium Medicinae," 240). The textbook was a compendium of Salernitan, Muslim and contemporary Christian medicine, and the first edition of Bernard's revision appeared in print on 20 May 1480. For Bernard, linked by Chaucer in the *General Prologue* of the *Canterbury Tales* with two other contemporary physicians, "Gatesden, and Gilbertyn" (434), known to his physician pilgrim, the signs of lovesickness occur when patients "neglect sleep, food, and drink and when their whole body except for the eyes is weakened and they have deep hidden thoughts with sad sighs."[12] Not surprisingly, since mania is always cited by the medical authorities as the prognosis for lovesickness, Bernard lists sleep among the prescribed cures for it: "anything that produces moistening is useful in the cure since the disorder comes about because of dryness; therefore, it is appropriate to use sleep, rest, idleness."[13] To Sarton, Chaucer's linking together Bernard of Gordon, John of

Gaddesden and Gilbert the Englishman in one line "illustrates the accuracy of Chaucer's learning, for he could hardly have made a better choice, and the three men mentioned by him formed a natural group and (if he had mentioned them in the right order) a natural progression" ("Lilium Medicinae," 242). Later, in the early fifteenth century *Philonium* by Valescus de Taranta, sleeplessness continues to be cited as a symptom of both *amor hereos* and mania.[14] To sum up, then, it is clear from both Chaucer's *Book of the Duchess* and from the classical and contemporary medieval medical authorities that sleeplessness is a serious symptom of melancholy, as well as of the related subclass of melancholy, *amor hereos*, and of the disease into which *amor hereos* always develops: mania. Not surprisingly, in all cases, sleep is one of the vital cures.

READING

Another frequently discussed cure for melancholy is reading; the narrator's insomnia, it will be recalled, was the cause of his turning to Ovid's tale. In *Chaucerian Fiction*, the chapter entitled *"The Book of the Duchess*: The Kindly Imagination,"* Robert Burlin observes that the poem "differs from the later dream-visions in that we find the dreamer literally 'using' a work of fiction. The story of Seys and Alcyone, directly or indirectly taken from Ovid's *Metamorphoses*, serves therapeutically to divert the narrator from an insomnia induced by an imprecisely defined melancholy" (59). The narrator, unable to sleep, turns to an old romance because he thinks "it beter play/Then play either at ches or tables" (*Duchess* 50–51). Now the narrator can view someone else's sorrow—Alcyone's—made beautiful and distant by art, which allows him to sublimate and, perhaps, transcend his own sorrow. Such fables as the narrator turns to were intended by their creators to be reflected upon by those in need of counsel:

> And in this bok were written fables
> That clerkes had in olde tyme,
> And other poetes, put in rime
> To rede and for to be in minde,
> While men loved the lawe of kinde.
>
> (52–56)

We cannot evade sorrow, but we can assert our human nature through reflection. As Chaucer retells Ovid's tale, he enlarges on the sufferings of Queen Alcyone, separated from her husband, so that the narrator may concentrate on a loss other than, but similar to, his own:

> Such sorowe this lady to her tok
> That trewly I, that made this book,
> Had such pittee and such rowthe
> To rede hir sorowe that, by my trowthe,
> I ferde the worse al the morwe
> Aftir to thenken on hir sorwe.
>
> (95–100)

Ovid's tale deepens the narrator's understanding of his own sorrow. The tale of Alcyone's grief, her husband Ceyx's message in her dream—"I nam but ded" (204)—and her death, precipitated by the blunt, stunning news, offers a lesson about *the lawe of kinde*: sorrow must come to an end.[15] The husband's message is clear on this point, "farewel, swete, my worldes blysse!/I praye God youre sorwe lysse" (209–10). While the narrator empathizes with Alcyone's story, he does not come to terms with the fact of her sudden death. Chaucer, in fact, abruptly cuts off the story, omitting Ovid's reunion of the lovers after death as birds, and lets the narrator drop off to sleep without the Roman poet's happy ending.

The narrator's dream is itself a kind of fable, for, indeed, when he awakens he thinks to himself,

"Thys ys so queynt a sweven
That I wol, be processe of tyme,
Fonde to put this sweven in ryme
As I kan best ."

(1330–33)

That is, he will make of his dream something like Ovid's
tale of Ceyx and Alcyone. When the dreamer encounters
the sorrowing black knight in the dream, he finds him
beyond the consolations offered by life—he is not interested in the hunt—or by art:

Nought al the remedyes of Ovyde,
Ne Orpheus, god of melodye,
Ne Dedalus with his playes slye.

(568–70)

The black knight, whose name suggests a melancholic
condition, is like the dreamer; his sorrowing heart "gan
faste faynte" (488) and "his spirites wexen ded" (489).
Here, as in Froissart's *Paradys*, imitated at the beginning
of *The Book of the Duchess*, the connection between the
loss of a loved one and lovesickness is explicit. Moreover,
also like the dreamer, he wonders "how hys lyf myght
laste" (506), for "he had wel nygh lost hys mynde" (511).
For both the grieving dreamer and the black knight, "a
tale" becomes the path to gaining "more knowynge of
hys [the knight's] thought" (536–38). In reality, of course,
the conversation of the two within the dream framework
is literature. The black knight's account of his courtship
of the lady White memorializes his feelings about her
and is a kind of romance. His account of her appearance,
even if accurate, is conventional to romance literature,
specifically Machaut's *Remede de Fortune* and the
Jugement dou Roy de Behaingne:[16]

And goode faire White she het;
That was my lady name ryght.
She was bothe fair and bryght;
She hadde not hir name wrong.

> Ryght faire shuldres and body long
> She had, and armes, every lyth
> Fattyssh, flesshy, not gret therwith;
> Ryght white handes, and nayles rede,
> Rounde brestes; and of good brede
> Hyr hippes were; a streight flat bak.
>
> (948–57)

Not only is White's beauty like something out of a story-book, but so is her virtue. She is likened to the fabulous bird of legend, "The soleyn fenix of Arabye" (982) and, for her "debonairte" (986), to "Hester in the Bible" (987). Much of *The Book of the Duchess* grows out of the dreamer-turned-poet recording the black knight's description of his lost lady. His memory of her is already a fiction, caught in the images of his suffering mind. In the end, without any solution, religious or philosophical, to the problem of mortality, the black knight is able to say plainly, "she ys ded!" (1309). As Burlin so aptly summarizes, "in purely human terms: the perceptive powers of the imagination in intimate cooperation with memory bring about a release from the paralysis of sorrow" (70). Interestingly, the imagination, over time an important element of the cure, is also an aspect of the disease, since, in love melancholy, it is the imagination that is affected, trapped by the image of the beloved so that the sufferer abandons all other bodily needs, including food and sleep. One could argue that the reading of Chaucer's narrator-dreamer strongly colors the contents of the dream, so that the preoccupations of the waking life are carried on in sleep. While the dream at first offers Ovidian coincidence of detail, it also gradually shows the way to escape.

The therapeutic effect of literature, especially in treating mental disease, was recognized by the ancients, and they continued to praise it up until Chaucer's day and beyond. Glending Olson observes of this poem, "however original and humorous Chaucer may be in describing his [the narrator's] means of falling asleep, it is worth noting that his invention in the *Book of the Duchess* seems predicated on a psychology of reading and sleeping that is explained in the *Tacuinum*," a Latin manual on hygiene translated from the Arabic in the thirteenth century (87). Olson's quote from this work, however, indicates that it is no more than an item from a table on sleep: "*Confabulator*: a teller of stories should have good discernment in knowing the kind of fictions in which the soul takes delight" (82).[17] The idea of the therapeutic good of pleasurable reading is explicit enough, but, as we shall see, many other more learned and elaborated statements on "literatherapy" were abroad in Chaucer's day in the medical literature (and some of these embody ideas that still hold weight today).[18]

Among the many early physicians who give space to the importance of literary diversion is Paul of Aegina who, in discussing lovesick persons, comments that these are frequently "wasted" by physicians who misdiagnose their ailment and prescribe "quietude"; whereas, "wiser ones" who are more skilled at diagnosis advise, among other treatments, "spectacles and amusing stories" (*The Seven Books* 3.391).[19] Such entertainment is likewise prescribed for melancholy by Avicenna in his *Canon of Medicine*[20] and by Bartholomaeus Anglicus in *De Proprietatibus Rerum*,[21] and for both melancholy and *amor hereos* by Valescus de Taranta in the *Philonium* (fol. 11r and 13r). Clearly the idea that the pleasures of literary diversion gave melancholics relief had currency in Chaucer's day; it would have had to be a virtual commonplace to have sifted down into a manual on health such as the *Tacuinum*. But the appearance of the idea in Avicenna and Bartholomaeus Anglicus has added significance in terms of the interplay of poetry and science during the Middle Ages, because Chaucer could easily have encountered their works.

Avicenna was readily available, and we know Chaucer was acquainted with his work, for in the *Pardoner's Tale* he mentions the distinctive chapter and fen divisions of the *Canon's* structure when he discusses the symptoms of poisoning:

> But certes, I suppose that Avycen
> Wroot nevere in no canon, ne in no fen,
> Mo wonder signes of empoisonyng
> Than hadde thise wrecches two, er hir endyng.
>
> (889–92)

J. A. W. Bennett, who considers Chaucer's learning unmatched by any other late medieval English poet, even though he never took a university degree, is persuaded that his interest in and proximity to Oxford and the rich holdings of the Merton College Library may have contributed to his achievements (12). As a lifelong servant of kings, Chaucer would have attended court at the palace of Woodstock, regularly used by Edward and Richard, which was eight miles to the north of Oxford and only accessible from London (where Chaucer lived) by passing through Oxford (Bennett, 18). The first appearance of Chaucer's name, in fact, occurs in the Woodstock household accounts for 1357. The poet associates his pilgrim clerk with Oxford, names two men with close ties to Oxford in his writing, "philosophical" Strode and Bishop Bradwardine, gives his tale of student life an Oxford setting, and credits his physician pilgrim with a knowledge of medical works so vast that he could not have owned them all . Bennett comments, "I can find no record of any collection containing them except Merton College" (15). If Chaucer himself spent time at Oxford, and if he went to the Merton College Library, one of the works he could have read there was Avicenna's *Canon*. The *Canon* contains a long section on signs of melancholy care, followed by a section on its cure. While emphasizing somatic cures such as bathing, drinking wine and being rubbed with aromatic oils, Avicenna also includes "listening to songs" in the context of such pastimes as hunting and sensual delights.[22] Equally accessible was Bartholomaeus Anglicus's *De Proprietatibus Rerum*, translated into Middle English by John of Trevisa in the fourteenth century. This encyclopedia also advises literary entertainment for the relief of those who are cast down—" þe remedye of þise is þat þe sike man be ileide in a ly3t place and þat þere be iangelinge and grete spekinge and disputesoun," "by swete voys and song[es] and armonye, acoord, and musik, sike men and mad and frenetek come ofte to hire witt a3ee and hele of body"—albeit of a distinctly oral, lyric nature.[23]

But by far the most detailed discussion of the therapeutic value of literary entertainment appears in Caelius Aurelianus's *Chronic Diseases,* as he considers cures for mania:

> ... have the patient read aloud even from texts that are marred by false statements. In this way he will exercise his mind more thoroughly. And for the same reason he should also be kept busy answering questions. This will enable us both to detect malingering and to obtain the information we require. Then let him relax, giving him reading that is easy to understand; injury due to over-exertion will thus be avoided. For if these mental exercises overtax the patient's strength, they are no less harmful than passive exercise carried to excess.
>
> And so after the reading let him see a stage performance. A mime is suitable if the patient's madness has manifested itself in dejection; on the other hand, a composition depicting sadness or tragic terror is suitable in cases of madness which involve playful childishness. For the particular characteristic of a case of mental disturbance must be corrected by emphasizing the opposite quality, so that the mental condition, too, may attain the balanced state of health. And as the treatment proceeds, have the patient deliver discourses or speeches as far as his ability and strength permit. And in this case the speeches should all be arranged in the same way, the introduction to be delivered with a gentle voice, the narrative portions and proof more loudly and intensely, and the conclusion, again, in a subdued and kindly manner. This is in accordance with the precepts of those who

have written on vocal exercise (Greek *anaphonesis*). An audience should be present, consisting of persons familiar to the patient, by according the speech favorable attention and praise, they will help relax the speaker's mind. (547–49)

A related cure in *The Book of the Duchess* is the process of "talking it out"—the backbone of current day psychotherapies—as exemplifed by the conversation between the black knight and the dreamer.

Talking

Years ago, at a time when some critics accused the dreamer of stupidity and lack of tact,[24] Joseph E. Grennen stated flatly, "The dreamer does clearly see himself in the role of physician" (138) and cited the supporting lines:

> But certes, sire, yif that yee
> Wolde ought discure me youre woo,
> I wolde, as wys God helpe me soo,
> Amend hyt, yif I kan or may.
> Ye mowe preve hyt by assay;
> For, by my trouthe, to make yow hool
> I wol do al my power hool.
> And telleth me of youre sorwes smerte;
> Paraunter hyt may ese youre herte,
> That semeth ful sek under your syde."
>
> (548–57)

Penelope Doob cites this passage as well and observes that the minor but very fine fifteenth century poet, Thomas Hoccleve, uses the same technique in the *Regement of Princes* (ca. 1412), wherein the poet depicts himself as a melancholic wandering in a state of distraction who has the good fortune to be found by a benevolent beggar (Doob, 217). This man insists on getting Hoccleve to talk with him and tell "the verray cause of þin hyd maladye" (262). Hoccleve is generally thought to be describing his own madness (Mitchell, 7–15), and Doob credits him with "considerable scientific and medical knowledge" (210). It is likely that Hoccleve is drawing on his personal experience combined with medical learning; there is also a strong probability that he is consciously reworking Chaucer's dialogue. Like the narrator in *The Book of the Duchess*, Hoccleve's beggar uses talk as a diversion from grief. Actually, as noted earlier, Chaucer's dreamer wants to establish contact with the bereaved knight even before the above-cited passage:

> Anoon ryght I gan fynde a tale
> To hym, to loke wher I myght ought
> Have more knowynge of hys thought.
>
> (536–38)

Far from stupid or clumsy, the dreamer's desire to intervene flows from his sense of the enormity of the black knight's grief,

> Hit was gret wonder that Nature
> Myght suffre any creature
> To have such sorwe, and be nat ded,
>
> (467–69)

gathered from tactful eavesdropping while the knight sange his "complaynte":

> "I have sorwe so gret won
> That joye gete I never non,
> Now that I see my lady bryght,
> Which I have loved with al my myght,
> Is fro me ded and ys agoon."
>
> (475–79)

The second half of the poem essentially relates the conversational give-and-take between the dreamer and bereaved knight, whereby the latter is enabled to express his sorrow directly to himself and another person. When, for instance, the black knight avoids the truth by losing it in the indirection of the figure of the chess game, the dreamer's conscious pose of obtuseness—"But ther is no man alyve her/Wolde for a fers make this woo!" (740–41)—gently prods the knight in the direction of unburdening his heart. As the dreamer well knows, the sorrow springs from the loss of a human being, and his remark opens the floodgates of memory. The bereaved knight spends some 300 lines detailing the beauty and virtues of his "lady dere" (720). After that space of recollection, the dreamer poses the unavoidable question, "Sir . . . where is she now?" which, briefly avoided, leads finally to the open confession, "she ys ded!" This frees the knight to return home to his castle and presumably to reenter the world of active living.[25] The "hert-huntyng" (1313) is done, heart's ease has been achieved, and the dreamer awakens thereafter with the book about "the goddes of slepyng" (1328) in his hand. By that point two mourners have been restored: the black knight of the dream is ready to resume the work of governance and the dreamer feels nearly ready to put the strange dream into "ryme/ As I kan best" (1332–33). It seems reasonable to view the second half of *The Book of the Duchess* as mostly detailing the progress of, as Robertson and Huppé so aptly put it, "the poet's discovery of his mourning self through facing its simulacrum" (53). This is a rather sophisticated development of one of the more frequent pieces of advice offered by early medical writers: that melancholics ought to get out and speak with friends.

Conversation of certain kinds is also described in treatments recommended for mania and *amor hereos*. Aretaeus of Cappadocia (ca. 150), a contemporary of Galen, concluded his chapter on melancholy (from *On the Causes and Symptoms of Chronic Diseases*) with the following account:

> A story is told, that a certain person, incurably affected, fell in love with a girl; and when the physicians could bring him no relief, love cured him. But I think that he was originally in love, and that he was dejected and spiritless from being unsuccessful with the girl, and appeared to the common people to be melancholic. He then did

not know that it was love; but when he imparted the love to the girl, he ceased from his dejection, and dispelled his passion and sorrow; and with joy he awoke from his lowness of spirits, and he became restored to understanding, love being his physician. (300)

Though Aretaeus includes this in a discussion of general melancholy, his account seems to be about what was later called *amor hereos*. Talk with the philosophical physician appears not to have uncovered the cause of apparent melancholy, but talk with the beloved reveals at once both cause and cure.

Thus talk, especially of particular types, is important in curing lovesickness. In a recently published, brief treatment of this disease, the *Liber de heros [sic] morbo*, Johannes Afflacius, translating the Arabic of a twelfth century north African physician (Ibn al-Jazzar), writes that "one of the better ways of removing thoughts of patients of *hereos* . . . is chatting with intimate friends" (Wack, 329). In the late thirteenth century *Lilium Medicinae*, Bernard writes more fully and specifically about the usefulness of talking in the cure of *amor hereos*:

> This kind of patient is either obedient to reason or not. If he is obedient, let him be removed from that false imagination by some man whom he fears and by whom he can be shamed by words and admonitions which would show him the perils of worldly living, the day of judgment and the joys of paradise.[26]

That is to say, have a friend talk him out of his folly. Lovers are notoriously secretive and refuse to talk as a matter basic to the whole diagnostic approach. Lovers have to be tricked into confession. Later on, in the same passage, Bernard urges the employment of "little old women" in the disparagement of the beloved: "as Avicenna says there are some people who enjoy hearing foul and forbidden things. Therefore go and get a hideous looking old woman with big teeth, facial hair, and disgusting clothing."[27] John of Gaddesden (ca. 1280–1361) repeats essentially the same advice in *Rosa Anglica*, "but in the cases of *amor ereos* it is necessary to speak contemptuously of the one he loves."[28] Those, however, whose dejected state has escalated to mania must not be crossed, even in conversation. Bernard, for instance, writes, "The first effective cure of all suffering from mania is joy and happiness because what does the most harm is anxiety and sadness and therefore their house should be bright and sunny and free of pictures and there should be many fragrant things there."[29] Then comes the relevant statement: "Everybody living in it should be attractive to look at. All those whom he is afraid of or whom he would be embarrassed to see if he had done something outlandish or done something foolish in their presence should be excluded."[30] The delicate state of those suffering from mania and the consequent sensitivity and tact needed in communicating with them is fully recognized, even in so early a treatment as Caelius Aurelianus's in the late fourth or early fifth century:

> . . . have the servants, on the one hand, avoid the mistake of agreeing with everything the patient says, corroborating all his fantasies, and thus increasing his mania, and, on the other hand, have them avoid the mistake of objecting to everything he says and thus aggravating the severity of the attack. Let them rather at times lead the patient on by yielding to him and agreeing with him, and at other times indirectly correct his illusions by pointing out the truth. (543)

According to this prescription for effective listening, the narrator of the *Book of the Duchess*—so willing to lead on the black knight with his *yielding* personality that some past critics thought him obtuse—may be seen as a masterful listener, even as viewed from the medieval physician's point of view. Such delicate therapeutic dialogues were all the more effective if conducted in pleasant locales. Typical testaments to the importance of place may be found in the *Liber de heros* [sic] *morbo* and in the *Lilium medicinae* where the matter is discussed in terms of lovesickness. Johannes Afflacius writes,

> Galen said: Talking with intimates removes a burden from the shoulders. If all these things—namely, drinking wine, music, and talking with friends—take place in gardens and meadows with flowing water, everything is altogether more delightful. But if gardens or meadows are lacking, let some delightful rooms be well strewn with flowers, roses, willow branches, myrtle, and basil. (Wack, "'The Liber de heros morbo . . .,'" 329)

Likewise Bernard of Gordon advises, "It is useful to change one's daily order and to be among friends and acquaintances and to spend time in places where there are lawns, fountains, mountains, shadey groves, pleasant odors, beautiful things to look at, the songs of birds, and the sounds of music."[31]

The placing, then, of the conversation of the black knight and dreamer is exactly right in terms of medieval medical thinking on *amor hereos* (a subject we will examine in more detail in the chapter on Chaucer's *Troilus and Criseyde*). The hunt passes and the dreamer tries to catch the friendly "whelp":

> And I hym folwed, and hyt forth wente
> Doun by a floury grene wente
> Ful thikke of gras, ful softe and swete,
> With floures fele, faire under fete,
> And litel used; hyt semed thus,
> For both Flora and Zephirus,
> They two that make floures growe,
> Had mad her dwellynge ther, I trowe;
> For hit was, on to beholde,
> As thogh the erthe envye wolde
> To be gayer than the heven,
> To have moo floures, swiche seven,
> As in the welken sterres bee.
> Hyt had forgete the povertee
> That wynter, thorgh hys colde morwes,
> Had mad hyt suffre, and his sorwes;

All was forgeten, and that was sene.
For al the woode was waxen grene;
Swetnesse of dew had mad hyt waxe.

(397–415)

The cyclic nature of human sorrow and joy is inherent in this natural landscape where "swetnesse of dew" has healed the earth of winter's cold and sorrows. Thus, just before the dreamer engages the black knight in artful conversation that eases sorrow and returns him to the active life of service, we are reminded of the seasonal cycles in nature and of the renewal which follows death. As Donald Baker comments on the passage, "All this, of course, is the ultimate 'moral' of the poem and the message to the Duke, John of Gaunt, that it is vain to mourn too greatly even for such a one as Blanche" (22).

On the basis of this examination of *The Book of the Duchess*, and in light of earlier scholarly discoveries about the interchange between medieval physicians and medieval poets, it appears that Geoffrey Chaucer knew well the medieval thinking and practices of his time, though it is impossible to ascertain how much of the medical writing he knew firsthand. But what, finally, can be said about the narrator's eight-year sickness? Is it *amor hereos*? melancholy? mania? Hill, as mentioned in opening this chapter, astutely observes that "One of the most prominent symptoms of love melancholy, fixation on the object of desire, is missing" (38). Chaucer's narrator emphasizes, rather, that "al is ylyche good to me—/ . . . for I have felynge in nothing," (*Duchess*, 9, 11), and that he is always dazed and dizzy. Hill's diagnosis of the disease is "head melancholy," a term borrowed from Robert Burton's *Anatomy*, which leaves the narrator "in danger of dying from default of sleep caused by his sorrowful *ymagynacioun*" (Hill, 41). It may be that there is only dazed numbness without fixation on the object of desire because White *is* dead: the ideal woman has become inaccessible forever. My own earlier comments on the poem in terms of *melancholia canina* would not, however, rule out *amor hereos*; indeed, that category of melancholy may embrace *hereos*. The tenth century physicians Rhazes and Haly Abbas are responsible for a loose association of *melancholia canina* with *amor hereos* that could lend support to the view that frustrated love is, indeed, the cause of the narrator's eight-year sickness. In Rhazes's *Continens*, for instance, he links the two categories of melancholy in a chapter heading: "Concerning Coturub."[32] But again, as the present examination shows, symptoms as well as treatments for lovesickness, melancholy and mania tend to overlap. The narrator's initial complaint of insomnia is a serious symptom shared by each of the three diseases. His recourse to reading Ovid is a sensible diversion that, again, is prescribed by early physicians for all three mental diseases. Moreover, the dialogue between the narrator and black knight, a benefit to both participants, is also in accord with treatments recommended for each of these diseases.

In the final analysis, a definitive diagnosis is not only hard to make but unnecessary, as lovesickness, melancholy and mania are not only perceived but treated in many of the same ways. Implicit in Chaucer's description of Arcite's mental condition in the *Knight's Tale* is the poet's understanding of the interrelationship of the three mental conditions—*amor hereos*, mania and melancholy. He says of Arcite's psychological state that it was

> Nat oonly lik the loveris maladye
> Of Hereos, but rather lyk manye,
> Engendred of humour malencolik
> Biforn, in his celle fantastik
>
> (1373–76)

It appears that Lowes began the scholarly journey from a very fruitful place.

Chaucer's passage on Arcite's mental state expresses a

psychological subtlety that suggests his comprehension of the extremes of human behavior went beyond merely being in touch with medical commonplaces of his day. It is, nonetheless, difficult to know just how much direct knowledge Chaucer had of the writings of that rather comprehensive list of medical authorities cited in the portrait of his physician pilgrim. In *Chaucer's Physician*, Huling Ussery discusses John of Arderne as a reasonable model for the physician, in preference to John of Gaddesden, who died too early (1349) to be a reasonable candidate (60–61). Chaucer probably had heard that "Peter de Barulo *alias* Master Peter de Salernia, physician" was arrested in 1387and may have been acquainted with one of his treatises. For all we know, this possibly unscrupulous man was a model for the physician pilgrim.[33] But such evidence does not make it possible to prove that Chaucer read the writing of medieval medical authorities; we are simply assured that it was not *impossible*. Rossell Hope Robbins, an indefatigable tracker of manuscripts, in his essay, "The Physician's Authorities," points out that in the fourteenth century, ten of Chaucer's authorities were among the 230 medical works in St. Augustine's Abbey at Canterbury; nine appear among 208 medical books in the fifteenth century catalogs of Christ Church, Canterbury; and all except two, Gaddesden and Rufus, are also found in the library of Dover Priory (341). Thus it was possible for Chaucer to consult medical treatises firsthand. Of course, the availability of texts only makes their reading possible, no more; I have never read *The Magic Mountain* though a copy is on a bookshelf in the living room. Yet over an over again, one senses behind Chaucer's verse not just the intuition of poetic insight but actual scientific learning. When, for instance, right before the dreamer offers his help to the Black Knight, Chaucer conveys the man's danger, expressing poetically his unnatural state of cold joylessness and nature's mechanism for correcting it, the poet does so in a way clearly informed by a knowledge of contemporary physiology. One hardly needs the evidence of parallel medical texts to feel convinced of a meeting of poetic vision and scientific knowledge in this passage:

> Hys sorwful hert gan faste faynte,
> And his spirites wexen dede;
> The blood was fled for pure drede
> Doun to hys herte to make hym warm—
> For wel hyt feled the herte had harm—
> To wite eke why hit was adrad
> By kynde, and for to make hyt glad.
>
> (488–94)

The ability of poets and physicians to see in parallel ways accounts for the ease with which they move in and out of one another's territory—not merely human nature, there for mutual viewing, but their works *about* that nature. This is even more apparent in the case of *Troilus and Criseyde*, Chaucer's preeminent discourse on desire and loss.

THREE

Chaucer's Troilus and Criseyde

Courtly Love and the Disease of Love

E ver since the term *courtly love* was invented at the
end of the nineteenth century, and even though serious questions have been raised about whether it describes anything that really existed in medieval life or literature, the term has been used to discuss a kind of love,
usually said to have arisen in southern France during the
twelfth century. It is characterized by certain ideas about
love between men and women—that illicit love must be
secret, that the mistress deserves the service, even wor-
ship, of her lover, that the lady's love enobles, and finally, that the price of such love may be pain, suffering
and sometimes even death.[1] About its various effects on
men and women, there is general agreement, but about

the origins of courtly love, controversy has raged long, remained unsettled, and is more or less peripheral to our concerns here.[2] I wish to focus attention on what is less well known: that many of these same ideas about the pain and suffering of love also appear in medieval medical treatises, where the phenomenon of much the same kind of love is treated as an illness, suggesting that there was, perhaps, greater similarity between the vision of medieval poets and physicians than there is between their modern counterparts. This is true even though what pragmatic physicians always cite in the signs of suffering as disease, proof of madness, poets sometimes see as indicators of lofty feelings and ideals.

Although some scholars have worked in both the history of medicine and the history of literature, not every point at which Aesculapius and Apollo meet has been studied as it deserves; one such point is that examined here, the medieval poets' portrait of what is commonly called "courtly love" and its relation to the medieval physicians' description of *amor hereos* (a subject that was briefly touched on in the previous chapter).[3] This chapter discusses the general features of *amor hereos* and some salient characteristics of the phenomenon known as courtly love as a prelude to its central concern, Chaucer's *Troilus and Criseyde* and the double view it offers of love: love as disease and love in its purest medieval form. The purest type of courtly love was, of course, that which omitted the final solace—the omission that caused all the pain and suffering written about by poets and physicians. Since courtly love was founded on desire, its frustration naturally became physically manifest. We see this poetically in Chaucer's Troilus and by definition in book 1, chapter 1 of Andreas Capellanus's *The Art of Courtly Love* (1277), where Andreas defines love as "inborn suffering derived from the sight of and excessive meditation upon the beauty of the opposite sex, which causes each one to wish, above all things, the embraces of the other and by common desire to carry out all of love's precepts in the other's embrace" (Capellanus, 2). If courtly love in its most ideal form were not so pure, so chaste, it would not be so painful.

Amor Hereos

With his usual wit and clarity, C. S. Lewis, in *The Allegory of Love*, reminds us of the need and the value of reconstructing Chaucer's intellectual background: "The stupidest contemporary, we may depend upon it, knew certain things about Chaucer's poetry which modern scholarship will never know" (163). A brilliant instance of recovery is John Livingston Lowes's demonstration that Chaucer's roll call of classical and contemporary medieval physicians, appearing in the portrait of his Canterbury-bound physician pilgrim, is no idle list ("The Loveres Maladye," 491–546). Studying the etymology of *hereos*, Lowes proved that the description of Arcite's physical and mental condition in the *Knight's Tale* parallels, almost word for word, descriptions of love sickness (*hereos*) found in medieval medical treatises. The implication of Lowes's discovery is that Chaucer built a character to accord with received notions about a specific mental condition. Until Lowes's article appeared in 1914, the meaning of *hereos*—the key to the whole description of Arcite's symptoms—had been misunderstood by every editor and commentator that referred to the term. With commendable caution, Lowes said that it would be difficult to know for sure if Bernard of Gordon's *Lilium medicinae* or John of Gaddesden's *Rosa anglica* were among Chaucer's "bokes old and newe," and he never followed his gleanings beyond the *Knight's Tale*, even though that was his intent. His *Modern Philology* article, nonetheless, stands as an eloquent testimony to, if not a demonstrable osmosis between treatment of the effects of excessive love in medieval literature and the *signa* of the medical books, then clear evidence, at least, that

medieval physicians and poets view the same phenomena in parallel ways. In the case of a poet such as
Chaucer, this means, at the very least, that his innate
perceptiveness alone might have made his vision of psychological disease as keen as any university-trained doctor's. However, that explanation seems insufficient to account for the learned nature of a passage such as Chaucer
wrote, for instance, describing Arcite's love-longing. Its
precision goes far beyond what innate psychological sensitivity could accomplish, and it is too accurate in terms
of medieval medical thinking to be explained completely
by root cultural conditions giving rise to parallel mani-
festations in medicine and poetry.

The appearance of the word *hereos* in Chaucer's description of Arcite's love for Emelye in "The Knight's
Tale" sparked Lowes's initial investigation:

> His slep, his mete, his drynke, is hym biraft,
> That lene he wex and drye as is a shaft;
> His eyen holwe, and grisly to biholde,
> His hewe falow and pale as asshen colde,
> And solitarie he was and evere allone,
> And waillynge al the nyght, makynge his mone;
> and if he herde song or instrument,
> Thanne wolde he wepe, he myghte nat be stent.
> So feble eek were his spiritz, and so lowe,
> And chaunged so, that no man koude knowe
> His speche nor his voys, though men it herde.
> And in his geere for al the worlde he ferde
> Nat oonly lik the loveris maladye
> Of *Hereos*, but rather lyk manye,
> Engendred of humour malencolik,
> Biforen, in his celle fantastik.
>
> (emphasis mine; 1361–76)

Lowes demonstrated that *hereos* had long been misread
as "Eros" or "heroes," and that etymologically the word
was actually a blend with roots in the Greek *eros*,
the Arabic *al-'isq*, and the Latin *herus*. He proved that
hereos is the scientific name for lovesickness and that

Chaucer's description of the malady suffered by Arcite is in accord with accounts of medical authorities. First, Arcite's symptoms follow medical physicians' descriptions closely:

His sleep, his mete, his drink is him biraft,	[The signs are when they lose sleep, food or drink—Bernard]
That lene he wex.	[And the whole body grows thin—Bernard]
His eyen holwe.	[And the eyes become hollow—Arnald]
His hewe falow.	[And their faces are yellowish from lack of sleep—Rhazes]
And waillynge al the nyght, makynge his mone.	[The *hereos* patients proceed to screech and cry out all night long—Rhazes]
And if he herde song or instrument, Thanne wolde he wepe.	His disposition is changed to sadness and tears when he hears love songs—Avicenna][4]

And the similarities between Chaucer's description and the medical view of *hereos* do not stop with anorexia, insomnia, hollow eyes, pallor, moaning and weeping. Chaucer's assertion, secondly, of a connection between *hereos* and mania is borne out by the medieval physicians. In Bernard, for example, the chapter on *hereos* follows that on mania and melancholy; in John of Gaddesden *hereos* is part of the discussion of mania and melancholy. The prognosis for lovers who are not cured of *hereos* is mania: "unless those suffering from *hereos* get help they fall into mania or die."[5] Third, and, finally, Chaucer's doctrine of the cells of the head is accurate in connection with *hereos* and mania:

Mania is an infection of the front cell of the head along with loss of the imagination. . . . Melancholy is sadness and fear and the destruction of speech; its location. . . . is the middle cell of the head between that of reason and fantasy.[6]

Chaucer, moreover, reveals his understanding of the tripartite anatomy of the brain by locating Arcite's imagination in the front chamber of the brain, "biforn in hys celle fantastik" (1376). Constantine the African (1020?– 1087) offers a description of the three ventricles of the brain which was standard from Galen's time onward and which escaped Lowes's wide net:

> . . . the operation of mind is threefold: first, fantasy; second, rational intellect; third, memory. And there are two parts of the brain, one the fore part, the other the rear. And the fore part is divided into two parts. . . . And two ventricles change the air in the fore part; hence and in this manner they give to the brain animal spirit so that it produces the senses of sight, hearing, smell, taste, and, once again, fantasy. Hence it passes to the place which is in the middle of the brain, which is the body. In its passage the already subtle animal spirit is more clean and clarified than the spirit which was in the fore part of the brain, so that it produces reason and intellect and is held in the head of the middle ventricle, which is between the fore and rear part . . . [The rear ventricle stores memory.][7]

Did Chaucer take his understanding of the brain's anatomy directly from Constantine? He certainly *could* have; in "The Merchant's Tale," for instance, Chaucer names a specific work translated from the Arabic by "the cursed monk, daun Constantyn" (1810) on sexual matters, "his book *De Coitu*" (1811).[8] What Chaucer says about old January's use of herbal concoctions as aphrodisiacs and Chaucer's placing the extramarital frolic in the pear tree—a presumed source of natural contraception[9]—suggests he knew the contents of the work. Even more significantly, Merton College, Oxford, owned Constantine's translation of the *Pantegni*, and his *Viaticum* was a textbook in medieval medical schools, among them,

Oxford's (Bennet, 15). The popularity of Constantine's *Pantegni* is reflected in the number of times Bartholomaeus Anglicus falls into phrases such as: "as Constantinus seiþ in *Pantigny libro 9 capitulo 2*" or "as Constantyne seiþ in *libro primo capitulo 24.*"[10]

According to discussions of faculty psychology in the medical treatises (particularly those written after Gerard of Berry's commentary on Constantine's *Viaticum*), the first stage of lovesickness is due to the corruption of the *virtus aestimativa*, the faculty of estimation, located at the top of the middle ventricle of the brain. It controls the *virtus imaginativa*, which in turn controls the concupiscible function. If the lover's desire for an unattainable love object is excessive, that desire can overwhelm the faculty of estimation and an obsessive desire for sexual gratification overthrow reason. As Arnaldus de Villanova explains,

> This passionate love as is clear from the relations of man and woman seems to be inflamed as the reign of reason is overcome on account of the extraordinary pleasure of intercourse.[11]

When the order of reason is corrupted, the hapless lover is willing to suffer heat, thirst, sleeplessness and all the other symptoms of *hereos* Chaucer outlined in his description of Arcite. The heat of *amor hereos*—closely associated with mania—is caused by the overheating of the vital spirit by a pleasing form. This vital spirit, in turn, generates heat in the animal spirit, which inflames the middle ventricle of the brain, the seat of the faculty of estimation. The inflammation of the faculty of estimation creates dryness in the *virtus imaginativa* (controlled by the *aestimativa*); Arnaldus continues his explanation:

> Since a firm retention of the forms can in many cases not be produced at all without dryness, it necessarily follows that the cerebral part of the imaginative faculty is necessarily dried out. This can be demonstrated from the things previously discussed; it seems too that there is a strong and frequent passage of the heat of the spirits to

the cell of the estimative faculty whence they flow to the area of judgment where they collect. The front part in which the imaginative part resides on account of the consumption of humors by the remaining heat of the spirits, remains necessarily drier and less humid than it was.[12]

The result is that the pleasing form of the beloved object, even after it may have left, becomes imprinted in memory to the extent that it becomes an obsessive presence. This fixation is a primary aspect of the pathology of the disease of love and, as we shall see, Chaucer seems to have understood its mechanism precisely. Whether his source was Villanova or some other related source we cannot be certain.[13]

COURTLY LOVE

In some sense, this kind of love introduced into literature by the troubadours of twelfth century Provence may be thought of as a literary variant of the medical phenomenon. For our purposes, the important element of *courtly love* is the conception of love as ever unsatiated, increasing desire that ostensibly moved the lover to acts of virtue and nobility as he sought the favor of the beloved, a mode of behavior never discussed in medical descriptions of *amor hereos*. Those who arrive at this exalted form of pure love can possess the beloved as an image, which in the diseased mind of the sufferer of *amor hereos* becomes an *idée fixe*. To a certain extent, the sufferer may be seen, in some instances at least, as a failed aspirant to the highest form of courtly love. As Alexander Denomy would have it, "It is a love wherein desire is a means towards an end: progress and growth in virtue, merit and worth" (*The Heresy of Courtly Love*, 23).[14]

In its purest form, courtly love aims at the union of hearts and minds and foregoes the solace of physical possession. The difficulty of the lover's achieving this exalted level of human love is reflected in some of the commonplace conceits and formulae of troubadour lyrics:

i.e., the idea of love as a sickness, the lover's fears about losing the beloved. Ideally, desire and yearning for one's lady was supposed to produce joy, but in his humanity the lover, more often than not, suffers the real pain of the earthbound. Denomy tends to pass over such expressions of feeling as are found, for example, in these lines from "When I See the Lark Moving" by the troubadour, Bernard de Ventadour:

> Alas! how much I thought I knew
> About love, and how little I know!
> For I can't keep myself from loving
> Her who'll give me nothing in return.
> She's stolen my heart and all of me
> And all herself and all the world;
> And after she robbed me, left me nothing
> Except desire and a longing heart.
>
> .   .   .   .
>
> And she doesn't care a bit
> That I love her, I'll never tell her of it.
> No, I'll leave her. I'll give her up.
> She's murdered me. As a corpse I speak.
> I'm going away since she won't retain me
> Downcast, to exile, I don't know where.[15]

James Wilhelm comments that the lover in this poem "was a passionate slave to love and did not behave right" (162). What was *wrong*, I suppose, was that the speaker was not spiritually able to achieve the highest possibilities of courtly love. In the concluding stanza of Bernard's "My Heart's So Full of Joy," one sees as well the implicit likening of romantic passion to the Christian Passion in the poet's reference to the lover's martyrdom:

> Messengers, go and run
> And tell my most beautiful one
> the pain and grief
> I've suffered—and the martyrdom.[16]

This is a far cry from the point at which the poem began:

My heart's so full of joy
everything loses its nature for me.

And why? "I could go outside without my clothes,/ Naked in my shirt,/Because my true love keeps me safe."[17] In the end, however, he has proved unequal to his own observation that "a man's a fool to lose measure" and looks for a golden mean to protect him from love's excesses.

The troubadour conception of love spread from Provence to other parts of western Europe, including Northern France, Spain, Germany and Italy. Even Dante, who in the *Divine Comedy* places idealized love within a religious, philosophical framework, was influenced by the lyric poets of Provence. The poignancy of their poetry lies behind the famous lines describing the sensual love that sprang up between the ill-fated Paolo and Francesca as they read together one day from a medieval romance:

> Love, which is quickly kindled in a gentle heart, seized this one for the fair form that was taken from me—and the way of it affects me still. Love, which absolves no loved one from loving, seized me so strongly with delight in him, that as you see, it does not leave me even now. Love brought us to one death.[18]

The unfulfilled desire of pure love may have been the courtly ideal, but, as Wilhelm points out, "Dante never confused the idealized rhetoric of romantic poetry with idealized behavior in external cultural history" (258). Paolo and Francesca share space with Semiramis, Dido and Helen of Troy.

Love, being a *passio*, the medieval physicians tell us, can lead one to a state of sickness, although, in essence, love is not a sickness. Difficulty arises only when the causes of love are "dispositions of body inclining towards such concupiscence either on account of some advantage of some necessity as is the case between man and woman with their venereal constitution or the humidity that causes titillation in the organs of generation."[19] Love as desire, then, arises when the body is in a hot, humid condition. However, Father Denomy demonstrates that from the point of view of the troubadours "love illicit and adulterous at least in aspiration though it may be, is the source of all good and of all virtue" (*Heresy*, 27). For the courtly lover, desire is love. It may be that the troubadours got their conception of pure love from the physician-philosopher, Avicenna, just as they certainly borrowed verse forms from Arabic poetry.[20]

For more than 60 years—that is, since the Spanish Arabist, Julian Ribera, suggested that *trobar* is a derivative of Arabic *taraba*, meaning "to sing" (especially poetry)—some scholars have become increasingly convinced that there was interaction between Romance and Arabic cultures, especially in northern Spain and Provence (Menocal, xi). And when, in 1948, Samuel Stern discovered lyric poems in a Romance vernacular—Mozarabic—some scholars even thought they expressed something like courtly love.[21] Certainly textual evidence of vernacular love poetry in a Romance language tied to Arabic tradition could not be dismissed, but scholars are by no means unanimous in the belief that there is a significant Arabic background behind the troubadours of southern France. In her recent book on the influence of Arabic poetry on the troubadours, Maria Menocal concludes only that if we say the Arabic "influence was only one of many . . . we gain in expanding our canon of medieval courtly love poetry by including texts that in critical ways parallel the poetry of Provence" (88).

Arabic thinking, apart from verse, may also have helped to shape the troubadour conception of love. The cultural supremacy of the Arabic world in the period before the rise of the troubadour lyric is a fact of history. Even if we could not argue that the troubadours were reading Arabic medical and philosophical treatises, it might still be true that they were strongly influenced by the culture and philosophy of the Arabs. From the tenth century on, Christian Europe absorbed Arabic scholarship and culture, which represented a more mature civilization than that of Europe (Boase, 62). One work that may have contributed to the development of the idea of courtly love in troubadour verse and beyond is Avicenna's *Treatise on Love.*[22] It assigned to the animal soul a role of partnership with the rational soul, whereby the desire for union with external beauty furthers the rational soul in its ascent to the absolute Good. Attraction to physical beauty, according to Avicenna, is only an impediment to union with the good if the rational soul fails to dominate the animal soul:

> If a man loves a beautiful form with animal desire, he deserves reproof, even condemnation and the charge of sin. . . . But whenever he loves a pleasing form with an intellectual consideration, in the manner we have explained, then this is to be considered as an approximation to nobility and an increase in goodness. For he covets something whereby he will come nearer to the influence of That which is the First Source of influence. ("A Treatise on Love," 221; cited by Denomy, *The Heresy*, 68)

Thus, for Avicenna as for the troubadours, human love may be made the source of nobility. Eventually, however, the courtly ethos moves away from the early writings of Avicenna and others, always privileging unattainable desire.

When we turn from a philosophical work such as Avicenna's *Treatise on Love* to his medical work, the *Canon of Medicine*, we again see the importance he gives to love in leading a fully human life. Avicenna's prescribed cure for *amor hereos*, when other remedies fail, is union with the object of desire:

> Knowing the object of the patient's love is one of the ways of curing him. The trick in learning this is to take his pulse while naming many names and repeating them over and over. Whenever there is a great variation in pulse rate on account of this recital of names, and the patient acts as if he has been slain by the mention of one

of the names, then test that name by saying it repeatedly, and it will become evident whether or not it is the name of the one he loves.... Furthermore, when no cure is found except joining the two together with the blessing of church and civil law, then let that be done.[23]

When preoccupation with the beloved has gone beyond rational measure, only the loved one can provide the cure. Avicenna's view that coitus is the cure for the disease could not be more remote from the courtly ethos. It is animated by the practical view that physical coupling can save the patient's life—precisely the attitude behind the doctor's advice in Shakespeare's *The Two Noble Kinsmen*, a reworking of Chaucer's "Knight's Tale":

> Please her appetite,
> and do it home; it cures her ipso facto
> The melancholy humour that infects her.
>
> (5.2.37–39)

Love in *Troilus and Criseyde*

In her contribution to the C. S. Lewis *festschrift*, "*Troilus and Criseyde*: A Reconsideration," Elizabeth Salter reminds us of Lewis's overall view of the *Troilus*: "a great poem in praise of love" (86). Equal attention, I think, must be given to what Salter minimizes, calling it "the fretting urgency of love" (86). Though the poem contains the "suffisaunce" of book 3, the first two books recount Troilus's pains of unrequited love, while the last two give an account of his separation from Criseyde. A. C. Spearing has likened the architectural design of the work to "a great classical pediment," tracing a pattern of rise from a low, followed by a fall from a highpoint (*Readings*, 117–18). As Winthrop Wetherbee has emphasized in his recent *Chaucer and the Poets*, "The overwhelming sense of Books Four and Five is that "Troilus comes at last to stand alone" (205). The primacy Chaucer gives to the actuality of aloneness in love, more than anything

else, makes the poem a tragedy and anticipates Shakespeare's emphasis on the inescapable forces of separation
that would divide lovers in his play, *Troilus and Cressida. Amor hereos* is the disease of those who love alone
par excellance; this section of the chapter will explore
parallels between Chaucer's description of his character's
sufferings and the conventional discussions of the *signa*
of *amor hereos* in medieval medical treatises.

Early in book 1 of the *Troilus*, the hero is overcome
with love for Criseyde,

> His eye percede, and so depe it wente,
> Til on Criseyde it smot, and ther it stente.
>
> And sodeynly he wax therwith astoned,
> And gan hir bet biholde in thrifty wise.
> "O mercy, God," thoughte he, "wher hastow woned,
> That art so feyr and goodly to devise?"
> Therwith his herte gan to sprede and rise,
> And softe sighed, lest men myghte hym here.
>
> (1.272–79)

Troilus is a king's son, one of those with the means, station and leisure to fall in love as he does. Though a battle
was on, Chaucer makes it as easy to forget for the reader
as it is for Troilus. As the poet writes some 30 lines before Troilus's eyes are struck by Cupid's darts,

> strengest folk ben therwith overcome,
> The worthiest and grettest of degree:
> This was, and is, and yet men shal it see.
>
> (1.243–45)

The social class in which Chaucer places the brand of
love Troilus will suffer is traditional, named in medical
treatises *amor hereos* from the eleventh to the seventeenth centuries. To my knowledge, the term does not
turn up in any texts except Latin medical texts after the
fifteenth century. Thereafter a variety of rough syno-
nyms are used: heroic love, love melancholy, lovesickness, erotic melancholy, hero's melancholy, etc. By 1285

Bernard of Gordon, mentioned in Chaucer's roll call of physicians in the *General Prologue*, was a famous professor of medicine at Montpellier and a colleague of Arnald de Villanova. His *Lilium medicinae* contains a noteworthy passage on the term *hereos* in connection with the typical station of the disease's sufferers:

> [WHY THIS PASSION IS CALLED *HEREOS* BY SOME] It is called *hereos* because the noble [*hereosi*] and well born are accustomed to incur this suffering as a result of their abundant indulgences in pleasures, as Viaticus says: As happiness is the ultimate pleasure, so *hereos* is the ultimate pleasure, and to the extent that people lust, to that extent they become insane. One may compare what Ovid says: "From a high beam a sad weight hung."[24]

More succinctly, in the seventeenth century, Felix Platter and Danielus Sennertus state (respectively): "They call this species of dementia by the name *HEREOS* because it is customarily supposed to befall heroes, or great personages,"[25] and "love in Greek is *eros* from which the Barbarians name this disorder *Hereos*, and those afflicted with it *Heroticos*" (cited by Lowes, 535). In *The Anatomy of Melancholy*, Burton is ampler in the passage closing "Love, or Heroical Melancholy, his definition" (Part. 3, Sec. 2, Mem. 1, Subs. 2):

> It rageth with all sorts and conditions of men, yet is most evident among such as are young and lust, in the flower of their years, nobly descended, high fed, such as live idly, and at ease; and for that cause (which our Divines call burning lust) this mad and beastly passion, as I have said is named by our physicians Heroical Love, and a more honourable title put upon it, Noble Love, as Savanarola styles it, and are so ordinarily affected with it. (Dell and Jordan-Smith, 657)

It is not surprising, therefore, to find among Bernard's cures for the patient afflicted with *amor hereos* the advice, "let his leisure be taken away from him as from the person of whom Ovid says 'If you take away his leisure, the darts of Cupid perish.'"[26]

One reason leisure is necessary for the sickness to take root is that a principal feature of the disease is fixation upon the beloved. The early physicians tell us that persons suffering from *amor hereos* become so obsessed with thoughts of the beloved object that they are unable to do anything else but be lost in reverie. George Lyman Kittredge once objected "Nothing can be more absurd than to describe Chaucer's Troilus as a 'lovesick boy'. . . . The sufferings of Troilus are in complete accord with the medieval system. Lovers were expected to weep and wail, and to take to their beds in despair" (*Chaucer and his Poetry*, 122–23). Not only is Troilus a "lovesick boy," *pace* Kittredge, according to the code of courtly love, but also, judging by the clinical descriptions of patient symptoms by the physicians, a fairly typical sufferer of lovesickness as it was understood in Chaucer's day and for several centuries afterward. Chaucer takes pains to describe at length Troilus's obsessed anxiety with thoughts of Criseyde. First, in book 1, Troilus is so caught up in thinking of Criseyde that he can hardly stand up, and he comes near to hallucinating in visualizing her:

> And whan that he in chambre was allone,
> He doun upon his beddes feet hym sette,
> And first he gan to sike, and eft to grone,
> And thought ay on hire so, withouten lette,
> That, as he sat and wook, his spirit mette
> Right of hire look, and gan it newe avise.

> Thus gan he make a mirour of his mynde,
> In which he saugh al holly hire figure,
> And that he wel koude in his herte fynde.
> It was to hym a right good aventure
> To love swich oon, and if he dede his cure
> To serven hir, yet myghte he falle in grace,
> Or ellis for oon of hire servantz pace.

> (1.358–71)

This is that "fixation on the object of desire" missing from *The Book of the Duchess*. By book 3, Chaucer actually suggests that Troilus's strong desire to win his lady's favor has caused his thoughts to become "diseased":

> for the more part, the longe nyght
> He lay and thoughte how that he myghte serve
> His lady best, hire thank for to deserve.

> Nil I naught swere, although he lay ful softe,
> That in his thought he nas somwhat *diseased*,
> Ne that he torned on his pilwes ofte,
> And wold of that hym missed han ben sesed.
>
> (emphasis mine, 3.439–45)

But it is obvious even earlier that Troilus suffers with the lover's malady. Who should know better than Pandarus, who himself has been carrying on a hapless love affair in courtly fashion for years? Pandarus is afraid that if he does not get involved with his friend's problem, Troilus will die. From the beginning, Pandarus thinks in physicianly terms; early in his strategy for discovering the name of Troilus's love, he alludes to "Phebus, that first fond art of medicyne" (1.659). He clearly sees himself as a doctor operating in parallel to the traditional Avicenna pulse-taking trick (see pp. 77–78). He promises his friend not to betray him, even if his beloved "were Eleyne/That is thi brother wif" (1.677–78). Shortly thereafter he promises that he would even deliver up his sister to Troilus, if she were the cause of his painful longing—"by my wil she sholde be thyn to-morwe" (1.860–61). The suggestion of physical satisfaction—"Look up, I seye, and telle me what she is/Anon, that I may gon about thy nede" (1.862–63)—finally prompts Troilus's confession: "Criseyde!" (1.874).

It is true that Pandarus's nature inclines him to meddle. However, given his observation of Troilus's strange behavior, Pandarus, in his adopted role as doctor, is justified in thinking that if he does not intervene, the prognosis in Troilus's case will be death:

> longe he ley as stylle as he ded were;
> And after this with sikynge he abreyde,
> And to Pandarus vois he lente his ere,
> And up his eighen caste he, that in feere
> Was Pandarus, lest that in frenesie
> He sholde falle, or elles soone dye;
> And cryde "Awake!" full wonderlich and sharpe;
> "What! slombrestow as in a litargie?"
>
> (1.722–30)

Within the context of such pain, Troilus's questioning the paradoxical nature of love in his *Canticus Troili* seems, in retrospect, especially poignant: "If love be good, from whennes cometh my woo?" (1.402).

Early physicians seem to offer an answer, at least a partial one, with regard to excessive care. Paul of Aegina, who greatly influenced Arabic physicians, said "care is a passion of the soul occasioned by the reason's being in a state of laborious emotion. . . . they [lovesick persons] think of nothing but love, the affection is difficult to remove" (*The Seven Books* 1.390–91).[27] The Arabic physicians demonstrate remarkable insight into the compulsive nature of the lover's excesses. Lowes cites a passage from Ad-Damiris' *Hayat al Hayawan* elaborating the diseased quality of the lovesick patient's ruminations:

> This state [passion] gains in strength, and becomes ardent and excessive love (*al-ishk*), which is excessive love beyond bounds to such an extent that the imagination of the ardent lover is never free from the object of his love, and consideration and remembrance of the object of love are never absent from his thoughts and mind; the mind is diverted from the promptings of sensual energies, and the lover is prevented from eating and drinking. . . . and also from thinking, remembering, imagining, and sleeping. . . . When ardent love becomes strong, it becomes love-madness. . . . in which state there is no room left in the mind of the lover for anything but the picture of the object of his ardent love. (517)

Bernard's words in *De Passionibus Capitis* are very close

to the Arabic view. He begins by briefly stating the main cause—"That love which is called *hereos* is melancholic worry over the love of a woman"[28]—and then amplifies his idea:

> The cause of this suffering is impairment of the estimative faculty on account of a fixation on a figure and face. Hence when someone is madly in love with a woman, his mind is so full of her figure, face, and manner that he is convinced that she is better, more beautiful, more admirable, more attractive, more naturally endowed, and more morally endowed than any other woman, and therefore he burns with boundless desire for her and believes that if he could attain his goal of possessing her, that would be his happiness and bliss. In proportion to the extent that his judgment is impaired he thinks continually of her, neglects everything that he is doing, and, if anyone talks with him, understands scarcely any other subject of conversation except her. And because he is continually meditative, his worry is called melancholic.[29]

Valescus of Taranta, who, like Bernard of Gordon, taught at Montpellier, simply writes in his *Philonium* (1418), under the heading "*De amore hereos*," "the souls of lovers are day and night in a state in which they cannot effectively imagine anything else. God only knows how the reason works at times like that."[30]

Chaucer, very early, endows Troilus with other features discussed by the physicians. First, by the midpoint of book 1, the narrator explicitly states that obsessive love for Criseyde causes Troilus to let all other matters go by:

> So muche, day by day, his owene thought,
> For lust to hire, gan quiken and encresse,
> That every other charge he sette at nought.
> Forthi ful ofte, his hote fir to cease,
> To sen hire goodly lok he gan to presse;
> For therby to ben esed wel he wende,
> And ay the ner he was, the more he brende.
>
> (1.442–48)

Second, his anxiety over the object of his love keeps him from eating and sleeping, a characteristic mentioned by Ad-Damiris and discussed by many other early physicians. Bernard, for instance, notes among the symptoms of *amor hereos*, that the patients "neglect sleep, food, and drink,"[31] and earlier, Paul of Aegina writes of the lovesick, "Such persons" are "desponding and sleepless" (*The Seven Books*, 1.391).[32] Chaucer describes Troilus's state similarly,

> And fro this forth tho refte him love his slep,
> And made his mete his foo, and ek his sorwe
> Gan multiplie, that, whoso tok kep,
> It shewed in his hewe bothe eve and morwe.
> Therfor a title he gan him for to borwe
> Of other siknesse, lest men of hym wende
> That the hote fir of love hym brende.
>
> (1.484–90)

Chaucer's adaptation of Petrarch's sonnet, which stands apart from the narrative of book 1 as the *Canticus Troili*, fully captures Troilus's sense that his love has left him in an irrational state, one he is yet rational enough to be intensely aware of. His first words spoken as a lover, once he has left off his pretense of scoffing at love are:

> If it [love] be wikke, a wonder thynketh me,
> When every torment and adversite
> That cometh of hym, may to me savory thinke,
> For ay thurst I, the more that ich it drynke.
> "And if that at myn owen lust I brenne,
> From whennes cometh my waillynge and my pleynte?
> If harm agree me, wherto pleyne I thenne?
> I noot, ne whi unwery that I feynte.
> O quike deth, O swete harm so queynte,
> How may of the in me swich quantite,
> But if that I consente that it be?
>
> "And if that I consente, I wrongfully
> Compleyne, iwis. Thus possed to and fro,

Al sterelees withinne a boot am I
Amydde the see, bitwixen wyndes two.

(1.403–17)

Though in the song above the notion of courtly love as
the highest possible good is nowhere demonstrated, Chaucer does make clear by the end of book 1 that Troilus's
love for Criseyde has had some influence for the good,

For he bicom the frendlieste wight,
The gentilest, and ek the mooste fre,
The thriftiest and oon the beste knyght
That in his tyme was or myghte be;

(1.1079–82)

But, viewing the poem as a whole, it would be hard to
maintain that Troilus is ennobled by his love for
Criseyde, who is ultimately unfaithful to him.

Mary Wack, who argues that the medical view of *amor
hereos* provides Chaucer "with a materialistic, determin-
istic, and ethically neutral view of love," sees Criseyde
simply as "a cure for Troilus's lovesickness" ("Lovesickness in *Troilus*," 55). The erotic highpoint of the con-
summation in book 3, considered from this perspective,
is reduced to "a night in therapeutic intercourse with
Criseyde," on the order of what Masters and Johnson
might have arranged for a patient in search of sexual
therapy (58). This situation would seem to make a love
poem captive to—rather than based on—the medical
model. But as Wack rightly points out, Pandarus views
himself as a physician who is, indeed, making necessary
arrangements to save a friend's life: "oonly for t'abregge
that distresse,/For which wel neigh thow deidest as me
thoughte" (3.262–63). The medical paradigm whereby
Criseyde becomes therapy for sick Troilus presumably
removes the love affair from the realm of moral ethics.
Wack is certainly correct in singling out sexual intercourse as a recommended cure for *amor hereos* according
to medieval physicians, though it is not always given the
primacy she suggests. Bernard of Gordon and John of

Gaddesden, for example, discuss sexual intercourse only *after* other somatic cures such as drinking wine, engaging in conversation, taking baths and enjoying pleasant walks. Bernard, paraphrasing Galen, states the medical commonplace: "Intercourse . . . because it produces happiness and warmth and induces good digestion is therefore suitable for those *for whom it is permitted*" (italics mine).[33] I select this reference partly to indicate that medieval physicians are not uniformly neutral about the ethics of this cure. It is not all the same to Bernard whether or not the cure is used. Gaddesden, on the other hand, simply says, "moderate intercourse is recommended by some for expelling mania from the brain."[34] Whatever John of Gaunt's behavior actually may have been after the death of Blanche, nothing like this cure is even hinted in *The Book of the Duchess*. And it is unimaginable that it would be. Later, Christian physicians refused to follow Avicenna in his emphasis on the efficacy of coitus as a cure for *amor hereos*, preferring pharmaceutical and even surgical cures, but, as Donald Beecher wittily observed, this makes for bad plots. Juliet, after all, began as the woman who drove out Rosaline when Romeo's friend suggested crashing her party early in Shakespeare's play, at a point when Romeo was suffering from love melancholy.

According to Wack, progress is marked in Chaucer's tale by Troilus's movement from the point where he regards Criseyde, as Pandarus does, as a remedy for lovesickness, to a later position in books 4 and 5 wherein he transcends the material, medical view of love ("Lovesickness in *Troilus*," 59). Troilus emphatically refuses Pandarus's conventional physicianly advice to put the lost love of Criseyde "out of remembraunce" (4.393–96) by substituting a new love: "This lechecraft, or heeled thus to be,/Were wel sittyng, if that I were a fend" (4.436–37). Wack's argument that in the latter part of the poem Troilus gets sufficiently beyond his body, so that the urgency of lovesickness can no longer *determine* his behavior, allows one to go even further to add, in the language of the other theory of love—courtly love—that Troilus, by the end of the poem, has ascended to "pure love," in the troubadour sense. As evidence, one can do no better than cite the very lines Wack refers to in which Troilus addresses Criseyde, "whan myn herte dieth,/My spirit, which that so unto yow hieth,/Receyve in gree, for that shal ay yow serve;/Forthi no fors is though the body sterve" (4.319–22). Troilus's spirit remains faithful to Criseyde even in the face of her betrayal of their love. The authenticity of the feeling that rings through his lines in book 5—"I ne kan nor may,/For al this world, withinne myn herte fynde/To unloven yow a quarter of a day!" (5.1696–98)—sustains the force of the love story against the obligatory and disturbing countermovement Chaucer introduces in the final stanzas of the poem. No love ruled by Venus could, in medieval times, be made to lead to lasting happiness, because it is not through the mutable, as Boethius had convinced Chaucer and his contemporaries, that one finds happiness. Even if Chaucer had wanted to somehow reunite Troilus and Criseyde after she had gone to the Greek camp and there betrayed Troilus, the poet was not free to alter the ending of the inherited Trojan legend.

In embracing fickle Criseyde, according to the orthodox view, Troilus embraces mutable Fortune, which cannot last. By the end of book 5, Troilus does repudiate the pursuit of pleasure—"The blynde lust, the which that may not laste" (5.1825)—in favor of *the* Physician who "best to love is, and most meke" (5.1847), and so exchanges the goddess of Love for a loving God. It may be difficult for some readers to believe the palinode, but it is interesting that Charles Muscatine, who has recently published an essay reviewing the history of critical accessments of Chaucer's religious attitudes, has pointed out that the early Chaucer scholar, Thomas Lounsbury, one of the first to argue plausibly that Chaucer was *not* especially religious and became increasingly less so in the course of his career, considered "the apostrophe to the Trinity at the end of the *Troilus*" as "the height of his early, relatively religious phase" ("Chaucer's religion," 251). Moreover, Muscatine himself cites the conclusion of the poem, beginning from line 1835, as "the greatest" among the "great and religiously moving moments in Chaucer" (253). That the orthodox turnabout is uncongenial to Chaucer has been most persuasively argued both by Donaldson in his examination of the poetry of book 5 from line 1750 onwards, and by Salter in her consideration of the tension between authority and imagination.[35] It seems to me that one is convinced by the power of the love story that Troilus is in the upper spheres gazing down at the earth, laughing at those who mourn his death in battle, because that hallowed place is the just reward of those who love nobly on earth. Like Dante, who traveled through hell before arriving at paradise, Troilus won his perspective after passing through the depths. Indeed, Troilus's laughter recalls the Dante of *Paradiso* (22.133–35) who says, "with my sight I returned through every one of the seven spheres, and I saw this globe such that I smiled at its paltry semblance."[36]

This evidence suggests the medical tradition of *amor hereos* is an integral part of the imaginative structure of *Troilus and Criseyde*, enough so that this work may be said to reflect the way medieval medicine, literature and the ordinary human experience of loss and grief may come together in mutually illuminating ways. Chaucer's grasp of medieval medicine was technically sound with respect to melancholy, *amor hereos* and mania, seeming to suggest that he had direct knowledge of some medical texts.[37] It can be assumed, furthermore, that as a prominent poet and civil servant close to the royal family, Chaucer's position kept him in touch with the main currents of medieval intellectual life and culture generally; medicine was part of this continuity of medieval views.

To this we may add the certainty that a poet such as Chaucer and the best trained, most insightful physicians of an earlier age could see some of the same aspects of the human psyche and capture them in the distinctive languages of narrative poetry and medical prose. Finally, this examination may suggest that people of the medieval period were more passionate than has been generally thought.

SHAKESPEARE'S *TROILUS AND CRESSIDA*

Shakespeare's play of a shared story deserves some comment before we take leave of Chaucer's *Troilus and Criseyde*. Important evidence of melancholy as an issue in Shakespeare's *Troilus and Cressida* is Troilus's acute awareness of the problem of time, a melancholic theme as well in *As You Like It*. In some measure, the originality of Shakespeare's version of the story of Troilus and Cressida consists in the prominence he gives to time as a force of separation. The playwright's sense that the problem of time is of primary importance may be viewed as a genuine contribution to Renaissance understanding of the phenomenon of melancholy, for one does not encounter preoccupation with time listed among its symptoms in the early medical treatises. This absence is all the more surprising as, even common sense would suggest that, at the very least, time has something to do with love melancholy; the separation of lovers occurs *in time*. Perhaps it is for the poet to speak of the obvious. Almost everyone agrees that the real subject of the sonnets published in 1609 is time more than love. No collection of Shakespeare's poems would be complete without sonnets 12 ("When I do count the clock that tells the time") and 15 ("When I consider everything that grows/ Holds in perfection but a little moment").

Shakespeare has made his Troilus acutely sensitive to and passionate about *time*. In act 4, for example, to Cressida's bewildered question, "And is it true that I

must go from Troy?" (4.4.30), Troilus answers with powerful words:

> And suddenly, where injury of chance
> Puts back leave-taking, justles roughly by
> All time of pause, rudely beguiles our lips
> Of all rejoindure, forcibly prevents
> Our lock'd embrasures, strangles our dear vows
> Even in the birth of our own laboring breath.
> We two, that with so many thousand sighs
> Did buy each other, must poorly sell ourselves
> With the rude brevity and discharge of one.
> Injurious time now with a robber's haste
> Crams his rich thiev'ry up, he knows not how.
> As many farewells as be stars in heaven,
> With distinct breath and consign'd kisses to them,
> He fumbles up into a loose adieu;
> And scants us with a single famish'd kiss,
> Distasted with the salt of broken tears.
>
> (4.4.33–48)

The harsh verbs of parting—"puts back," "justles roughly by," "rudely beguiles," "forcibly prevents," "stran-
gles," "Crams"—underscore the cruel action of time on
human relationships. Similarly, Troilus, earlier in the
play, succinctly voices his complaint against the boundaries set, by human nature and time, on the possibilities
for love:

> This [is] the monstruosity in love, lady, that
> the will is infinite and the execution confin'd,
> that the desire is boundless and the act a slave
> to limit.
>
> (3.2.81–83)

But despite his railing against the adverse action of
time, Shakespeare's Troilus is remarkably resigned to
Cressida's departure to the Greek camp. As E. Talbot
Donaldson would have it, Shakespeare's Troilus resigns
himself to her going "as immediately as ever did
Criseyde in Chaucer" (*The Swan at the Well*, 107).

Cressida's "I must then to the Grecians?" (4.4.54) begs for a solution from her lover, but all he has to offer is "no remedy." (4.4.55).

About what influence Chaucer's poem might have had on Shakespeare's play there is some disagreement. Shakespeare could have read Chaucer's *Troilus* in several editions of his works: Thynne's of 1532, or its 1542 or 1550 reprints, or Stow's of 1561, or Speght's of 1598. All of these contained Henryson's *Testament of Cressid*, in which the heroine deteriorates into a leper—the text appearing immediately after Chaucer's poem without any indication of the change in authorship. Hillebrand, the editor of the New Variorum edition of *Troilus and Cressida*, observes that "if Sh[akespeare] read Chaucer he did so rather casually, borrowing remarkably little, and giving nowhere evidence of that careful attention which he was wont to employ" with other sources (449). Robert Kimbrough essentially agrees, adding that "many subtleties of characterization and interior monologue would have been lost to Shakespeare because of the controverting influence on Chaucer's narrative of the 'epilogue' full of diseases and divine retribution" (27). Donaldson appears to stand alone in his belief that "Shakespeare had a profound understanding of Chaucer's poem," but then he is primarily concerned with the similarity of the instincts the two poets demonstrate in their sensitivity to the heroine (*The Swan at the Well*, 75). I suggest that as far as the overall treatment of the legend goes, Shakespeare uses it to explore the relationship of love and war, while in Chaucer the war is kept far in the background. Moreover, in Chaucer's *Troilus and Criseyde*, the pathology of love melancholy is of extreme interest to the poet, whereas in Shakespeare's play it is reduced to a rhetorical shadow of itself, as, for instance, in Troilus's first description of Cressida:

> I tell thee I am mad
> In Cressid's love; thou answer'st she is fair,
> Pourest in the open ulcer of my heart

Her eyes, her hair, her cheek, her gait, her voice,
Handlest in thy discourse, O, that her hand,
In whose comparison all whites are ink.

(1.1.51–56)

We have here pure Petrarchan convention, empty of
Galen and his kind.

It's not as if Shakespeare forgot whatever he knew
of Galen in this play; things medical are simply kept on
the periphery, as can be seen in an ugly interchange involving Pandarus, Helen and Paris. Pandarus converses
mockingly on the subject of love with the two lovers
who ignited the Trojan War, jesting in song:

"Love, love nothing but love, still love, still more!
For, O, love's bow
Shoots buck and doe.
The [shaft confounds]
Not that it wounds,
But tickles still the sore.
These lovers cry, O ho, they die!

(3.1.115–21)

Pandarus's cynicism prompts Paris's critical analysis of
the old man's character, and curiously Paris draws on the
Galenic theory of the humours to explain Pandarus's nature to Helen:

He eats nothing but doves, love, and that breeds
hot blood, and hot blood begets hot thoughts, and
hot thoughts beget hot deeds, and hot deeds is love.

(3.1.128–30)

Paris knows well ecstacy and the world of pimps and
whores. This scene serves to trivialize the subject of love
and contributes a nastiness of tone to the play which
most reader's find among Shakespeare's most bitter.

Its pervasive bitterness, while not a melancholy "issue," like the problem of time, is clear evidence of that
often-remarked dark mood in the text. G. B. Harrison's
introduction to the play relates it to *Hamlet*: "*Troilus*

and Cressida is the work of a man in the bitterest mood of disillusionment to whom the world has become 'a foul and pestilent congregation of vapors'" (972).

Hot blood affects not only Cressida's uncle, Pandarus, but her Trojan lover. Hector points to this when he asks Troilus,

> is your blood
> So madly hot that no discourse of reason,
> Nor fear of bad success in a bad cause,
> Can qualify the same?
>
> (2.2.115–18)

The most mature of Priam's sons here emphasizes the sensual, irrational, immature foundation of Troilus's love for Cressida. Like the Trojan War itself—and time, which lies beyond human control—the sensual basis of their love adds to its fragility. Here lies the key to the dark tone of the play. It is not just that Helen and Cressida may seem like whores, Pandarus a pimp, and Troilus, along with Paris, stupidly hot-blooded, which justify anger and bitterness, but that in the face of the occasions for mutual attraction between the sexes that life offers and then the all too common necessity for separations, men and women feel helpless before their fates. In Shakespeare's *Troilus and Cressida*, then, we do not encounter melancholy as pathology but rather melancholy as mood, or even attitude toward the human condition—perhaps even Shakespeare's own temperament in 1603, the year *Troilus and Cressida* was entered in the Stationer's Register.

FOUR

Shakespeare's
As You Like It

The Melancholy Jaques

In the preceding three chapters I have attempted to place literary texts—Chaucer's *Book of the Duchess* and *Troilus and Criseyde*—within a context of related medical writing in an effort to enlarge our understanding of medieval thinking about melancholy, as well as to shed more light on Chaucer's poetic sensibility and his learning. To this extent my enterprise is historical, but my focus has been on *texts* much more than their margins: how they resemble one another, influence one another, and function within a poetic framework. As I continue to pursue melancholy into Renaissance medicine and Shakespeare's plays, *As You Like It* and *Hamlet*, the movement in time may seem to produce a greater sense of continuity than of development. This probably testifies as much to what Lee Patterson has called

"transhistorical humanness" as to actual similarities between Chaucer and Shakespeare as poets or between the
medieval and Renaissance worlds' ways of seeing melancholy (Patterson, 17). If so, we have a measure of melancholy's worth as a subject for humanistic exploration. Far
from rendering it useless to employ a historical perspective or to examine poetic treatments of particular poets,
the ubiquitousness of melancholy makes it important to
understand in detail.

For all its vital energies, Elizabethan England did not
fail to furnish its greatest playwright with opportunities
to learn what melancholy was, and this knowledge
helped him forge in Hamlet the English theater's most
durable portrait of the melancholic man. Shakespeare
was interested in the melancholy humour, the melancholic and melancholy in general—78 times the word
melancholy or words built on its root appear in his
works.[1] His knowledge of the theory of the humours, it
has been demonstrated, comes from familiarity with contemporary medical theory (Campbell, Anderson). In having these interests, he was a typical informed man of his
time, and Hamlet—more than any other creation of
Shakespeare's—demonstrates the ideological potential of
basing a character on theories of melancholy. Before the
creation of Hamlet, Shakespeare produced in the comic
figure of Jaques something like a trial version. The play
in which he appears, *As You Like It*, was not published
until 1623, when it appeared in the First Folio. However,
the play had been written between June 1599 and August
1600—early enough to have been influenced by such
medical treatises as Thomas Elyot's *Castell of Health*
(1534), Andrew Boorde's *Breviarie of Health* (1547), the
English translation of Juan Huarte de San Juan's *Examen
de Ingenios* (*The Tryal of Wits*, 1575), Levinius Lemnius's *Touchstone of Complexions* (1576), Richard Surphlet's translation of André Du Laurens's *A Discourse
of the Preservation of the Sight* (1599) and that other
major late sixteenth century medical treatise, Timothy
Bright's *A Treatise of Melancholie* (1586), much in vogue

between 1586 and 1613. Publication of Robert Burton's *The Anatomy of Melancholy* and Jaques Ferrand's *Erotomania* at the end of the first decade of the seventeenth century came too late to have directly influenced Shakespeare's conception of Jaques.[2]

After examining a key passage in which Jaques describes what his brand of melancholy is and is *not*, this chapter proceeds to briefly review scholarly treatments of his melancholy. Three of these are, as far as I have found, unknown but among the earliest to address the subject. One, penned by a forgotten eighteenth century academic, is of interest because it pinpoints a question that would vex generations of literary commentators: is Jaques a mean-spirited cynic or a genial philosopher? The other two are especially noteworthy for our purposes, as they were written by nineteenth century physicians whose area of expertise was diseases of the mind; one of these even coauthored *the* textbook of the day on mental diseases. While the two physicians can tell us nothing about Renaissance medical views of melancholy, as pre-Freudian physicians of the mind, they do something none of the Renaissance writers on the disease do: they show us early medical practitioners commenting directly on the specific mental features of Shakespeare's Jaques, before the invention of psychiatry as we know it. The major task of this chapter, however, will be to explore the pervasiveness of melancholy in this early Shakespearean play and Jaques's vital position as a fulcrum around which move images and ideas associated with melancholy. Among these are: *the weeping stag, solitude, time, exclusion from love, travel—* images and ideas that have much to do with the literary tradition of melancholy in the sixteenth century. They may also be seen to combine with those ideas in Renaissance medical treatises on melancholy that culminate in Bright's treatise, generally recognized as having directly influenced Shakespeare's *Hamlet*, and Burton's *Anatomy*, published after Shakespeare's death.

Jaques's words to Rosalind are virtually his own

Anatomy of Melancholy, a description of the condition he evidently considers peculiar to himself, even, perhaps, unique:

> I have neither the scholar's melancholy,
> which is emulation; nor the musician's, which is
> fantastical; nor the courtier's, which is proud; nor
> the soldier's, which is ambitious; nor the lawyer's,
> which is politic; nor the lady's, which is nice; nor
> the lover's, which is all these: but it is a melan-
> choly of mine own, compounded of many simples,
> extracted from many objects, and indeed the sun-
> dry contemplation of my travels, in which [my]
> often rumination wraps me in most humorous
> sadness.
>
> (4.1.10–20)

Jaques's effort at accurately defining his individual type of melancholy, which rules out other kinds associated with other sorts of people, conveys Shakespeare's sense of the pervasiveness of melancholy among the creative (scholars and musicians), the political (courtiers), the professional (soldiers and lawyers) and the genteel (ladies and lovers), while at the same time permitting the play-wright to ridicule that pervasiveness a little. It perhaps even provides an opportunity to parody the elaborate classifications of the varieties of melancholy found in the popular medical treatises of the day. Jaques's use in this passage of the terms "simples" and "humorous," borrowed from such learned contexts, invite this con-clusion, which certainly fits the comic mood of the play as a whole.

Elizabethan psychological theory subdivided melan-choly into two main varieties: "natural" and "unnatu-ral." The disease was considered *natural* melancholy when the melancholic humour was normal in quality but excessive in quantity, and *unnatural* when the mel-ancholic humour arose from the burning (or "adustion") of any of the four humours. Elyot managed a simple statement of the idea in *The Castell of Helthe* (1539):

Melancolie is of two sortes, the one is called naturall, whiche is onelye colde and drye, the other is callyd aduste or burned: naturall melancoly is, as Galen sayth, the residence or dregges of the bloud: and therefore is colder and thicker then the bloud. Melancoly adust is in foure kynds, either it is of naturall melancoly adust, or of the more pure part of the bloud adust, or of choler adust, or of salt fleume adust. (110)

Very elaborate statements, however, such as that in Burton's *Anatomy* were more typical:

... melancholy is either simple or mixed; offending in quantity or quality, varying according to his place, where it settleth, ... or differing according to the mixture of those natural humours amongst themselves, or four un-natural adust humours, as they are diversely tempered and mingled. If natural melancholy abound in the body, which is cold and dry, "so that it be more than the body is well able to bear, it must needs be distempered," ... and so the other, if it be depraved, whether it arise from that other melancholy of choler adust, or from blood, produceth the like effects, and is. ... if it come by adustion of humours, most part hot and dry. Some differ-ence I find whether this melancholy matter may be en-gendered of all four humours, about the colour and tem-per of it. ... From melancholy adust ariseth one kind; from choler another, which is most brutish; another from phlegm, which is dull; and the last from blood, which is best. (Mem. 3, Subs. III, 173–74 [Ed., H. Jackson])

When Jaques says his own type of melancholy is "com-pounded of many simples, extracted from many objects" he appears to play with humoural classifications such as these. The particular terms "simple" and "com-pounded," however, also appeared in Elizabethan classifi-cations of the passions and their composition. Thus, Bright (1550?–1615), a physician very likely known to Shakespeare and about whom I will say more in the sub-sequent chapter, explains in his *Treatise of Melancholie*, "All perturbations are either simple or compounded of the simple. Simple are such as haue no mixture of any other perturbation" (82). The care with which Jaques distinguishes *his* melancholy from that of *others*, certainly marks him off as a posturer, but need not rule out the likelihood that he is, nonetheless, a genuine melancholic who is sad, as he says, because of the melancholic humour that is, in his case, somehow related to "rumination," "contemplation" and "travel."

Scholarly interest in Jaques's melancholy is longstanding and fairly consistent. Neglected but illuminating among the earliest commentators are William Richardson, an eighteenth century scholar from the University of Glasgow with the striking title, *Professor of Humanity*, and two nineteenth century physicians, John Charles Bucknill (1817–1897), who coauthored with D. Hack Tuke a respected nineteenth century textbook of psychological diseases, and A. O. Kellogg, assistant physician at what was known as the State Lunatic Asylum in Utica, New York.[3] In discussing Jaques's nature, Richardson begins by distinguishing between *melancholy* and *misanthropy*: "On comparing the sorrow excited by repulsed and languishing affection, with that arising from the disappointment of selfish appetites melancholy appears to be the temper produced by the one, misanthropy by the other. Both render us unsocial; but melancholy disposes us to complain, misanthropy to inveigh" (156). Terms thus clarified, he judges the character of Jaques to be a "mixture of melancholy and misanthropy," which renders him "more agreeable to human nature than the representation of either of the extremes" (156). Jaques also comes off rather well in John Charles Bucknill's evaluation of his personality:

> "The melancholy Jaques" is another phase of the Hamlet character, contemplated under totally different circumstances. There is the same contemplative cast of thought on the frailities of man exercising itself in obedience to a depressed state of emotion. In Jaques this has not been the result of sudden revulsion of feeling, of some one great grief, which has as it were, overspread the heavens

with a pall. It is of more gradual and whole-some growth, the result of matured intellect and exhausted desire. Jaques is an "old man," or at least old enough to be called so by the rustic lass in her anger of disappointment; and he himself indirectly attributes his melancholy to his wide knowledge of the world. (*The Mad Folk*, 292)

Bucknill's contemporary, Kellogg, also a physician, based his analysis of Shakespeare's Jaques on what he refers to as his long experience observing "the phenomena of mind as warped by the more delicate shades of disease,— shades so delicate perhaps as to be scarcely recognized" (87–89). He makes the point that mild yet very real cases of melancholia frequently contain what appear to be incompatible veins of genuine humor. Citing Jaques's own reference to himself as someone who is sometimes "wrapped in a most humorous sadness," the physician concludes that Jaques fits here as a character in whom "Shakespeare intended to represent a certain delicate shade of incipient melancholia." He quotes in full Jaques's act 4 description of his own brand of melancholy, and attempts to refine his diagnosis of the character's "gradual ingravescence of the melancholic state" by referring to a passage in Burton's *Anatomy*:

> "Generally," says Burton, "thus much we may conclude of melancholy, that it is most pleasant at first, *blanda ab initio*, a most delightful humor to be alone, dwell alone, walk alone, meditate alone—lie in bed whole days dreaming awake, as it were, and frame a thousand fantastical imaginations unto themselves; they are never better pleased than when they are so doing; they are in paradise for the time. Tell him what inconvenience will follow, what will be the event, all is one. *Canis ad vomitum*, 't is so pleasant he cannot refrain; so, by little and little, by that shoe-horn of idleness, and voluntary solitariness, melancholy that feral friend is drawn on." (Kellogg, 89)

In Kellogg's estimation, Jaques—*not* a genuine melancholic in whom one finds "a fixed condition of disease"—gets the best of what melancholy can offer: "he is . . . a most delightful dreamer, and the very prince of contemplative moralizing idlers; a species of intellectual and emotional epicurean. . . . Everything . . . which can . . . administer to his intellectual and emotional gratification . . . he converts . . . into a most delicious, healthful, and life-giving intellectual aliment . . ." (90). Melancholy in Jaques, according to Kellogg, does not become the poison that afflicts the morbid imagination of the "advanced" melancholic. Since Jaques represents just the beginning stages of the melancholy condition, Kellogg finds in him the "gentle satirist" (101). The only other physician, to my knowledge, who has written a full-length study of madness in Shakespeare is W. I. D. Scott, and he fundamentally agrees with his nineteenth century predecessors, especially Kellogg: "The character of Jaques in *As You Like It* is Shakespeare's own conception of the melancholy philosopher" (61), "Jaques is a critical student of human nature, decrying the pattern of organized society, but not without feelings capable of being moved" (64), "Jaques's conscious type is that of the thinking introvert" (65).

Jaques does not come off so well, however, in the first major study of melancholy by a literary scholar, Lawrence Babb. In his *Elizabethan Malady*, he emphasizes Jaques's moroseness, cynicism, rudeness, hate of "the infected world" (2.7.60) and labels him "the best example in the drama of the malcontent in the role of philosophic critic" (93). And, indeed, much of the criticism of the past 40 years is caught up in weighing the degree to which Jaques should be thought a mean-spirited malcontent or a genial philosopher—more or less the point at which Richardson began the scholarly discussion in the eighteenth century. The extremes are typified, on the one hand, by Helen Gardner, who views Jaques's cynicism as primary—he is "the cynic, the person who prefers the pleasures of superiority, cold-eyed and cold-hearted," (66–67)—and, on the other, by Erwin Panofsky,

who considers Jaques a true intellectual melancholic—
"A climax of refinement [of intellectual melancholy] is
reached in Shakespeare's Jaques who uses the mask of a
melancholic by fashion and snobbery to hide the fact
that he is a genuine one" (*Albrecht Dürer*, 1.166). Panofsky's idea is an interesting one and, as subsequent
discussion will demonstrate, there is evidence in the
play that Jaques's behavior fits Renaissance theories
about phlegmatic as well as choleric varieties of unnatural melancholy.

While it is impossible to imagine *Hamlet* without
Hamlet in the play, Jaques is neither central to the action
of *As You Like It* nor the play's hero. Hardin Craig put
the situation succinctly: "Jaques does nothing and is yet
indispensable."[4] Melancholy is crucial, I believe, to the
texture of this play, and around the figure of Jaques there
cluster images, ideas and themes intimately intertwined
with that mood. They are instances of what Stephen
Greenblatt labels "textual traces" that are central to literary interest in Shakespeare as "products of extended
borrowings, collective exchanges, and mutual enchant-
ments" (*Shakespearean Negotiations*, 7). They move
metaphors, emblems and items of clothing from one
zone of culture to another (7). The rest of this chapter
will explore these, some of which interconnect with
medical views found in sixteenth century treatises.

THE WEEPING STAG

Jaques's relationship to the weeping stag in act 2, scene
1, is the most potent touchstone of the importance of
melancholy to an understanding of his character. The
scene operates like a tableau on the subject of melancholy, as a lord in the Forest of Arden portrays the reso-
nance between Jaques, stretched out despondently beneath an old tree beside a brook, and the lone stag
weeping tears into its stream. The account captures in

poetic images what cannot be portrayed in dramatic action:

> To-day my Lord of Amiens and myself
> Did steal behind him as he lay along
> Under an oak, whose antique root peeps out
> Upon the brook that brawls along this wood,
> To the which place a poor sequest'red stag,
> That from the hunter's aim had ta'en a hurt,
> Did come to languish; and indeed, my lord,
> The wretched animal heav'd forth such groans
> That their discharge did stretch his leathern coat
> Almost to bursting, and the big round tears
> Cours'd one another down his innocent nose
> In piteous chase; And thus the hairy fool,
> Much marked of the melancholy Jaques,
> Stood on th' extremest verge of the swift brook,
> Augmenting it with tears.
>
> (2.1.29–43)

Further conversation between Duke Senior and the lord reveals that Jaques sympathized with the "poor deer" (47) for adding his tears to a stream that already had "too much" water and for being alone, "left and abandoned of his velvet [friends]" (50). It is significanct that the lord, in answer to Duke Senior's question, "But what said Jaques?" (2.1.43), replies that Jaques translated his feelings for the weeping, wounded deer "into a thousand similes" (2.1.45), for it was the opinion of Renaissance physicians of the day that the melancholic had great verbal skills. In *A Treatise of Melancholie*, Bright discusses the great wit of those who are melancholic, of the *adust*, burnt type:

> Sometimes it falleth out, that melancholic men are found verie wittie, and quickly discerne: either because the humour of melancholie with some heate is so made subtile, that as from the driest woode risest the clearest flame. . . . (130)

Earlier in the sixteenth century, Juan Huarte de San Juan, whose *Examen de Ingenios* was first published in 1575 and translated into English as *The Tryal of Wits*, wrote of the "great Understanding with a great Imagination," which made those "Melancholic by Adustion" such remarkable preachers because their imaginations furnished them "with Figures wherewith to Speak" (240). He cites an extreme case of the "fluent faculty" proceeding from heat in a melancholic man "who for more than eight days, spoke never a word, and then immediately fell into a fit of Rhiming, very often making no less than a good entire Stanza" (115–16). Similarly, Andrew Boorde emphasizes the imagination of the melancholic when he calls melancholia "a sickness fulle of fantasies" and cites as its cause "an euill melancholy humour . . . a stubberne heart and running to farre in fantasies" (78r). Clearly, Jaques's imagination has not turned him into a lunatic who has taken leave of reason; he is simply verbal and full of wit and capable of giving delight. For this reason, Duke Senior asks to be shown Jaques and the deer: "Show me the place./I love to cope him in these sullen fits,/For then he's full of matter" (2.1.67–69).

Presented as he is from the beginning of the play, beside a brook and weeping, Jaques seems to be melancholy because of the adustion of phlegm. The phlegmatic were generally thought to be attracted to water. André Du Laurens (1558–1609), Professor of Medicine at Montpellier and author of *A Discourse of the Preservation of the Sight*, translated into English by Richard Surphlet and published in London in 1599, observes that "the phlegmatike partie dreameth commonly of riuers of water" (95). Levinius Lemnius, in his *Touchstone of Complexions*, "Englished" by Thomas Newton in 1576, likewise writes that they "in Dreames imagine and thyncke themselues dyuinge ouer head and eares in Water, or be in Bathes and Baynes." (Lemnius, 112v). The scene ends with Jaques's reported "weeping" about the "sobbing deer" while commenting on the cruelty of the members of the court who, having settled in the forest, kill the native deer for food in their own home. When

Jaques sees a herd of deer run by the weeping stag he reportedly likens them to the indifferent masses of men found in "[the] country, city, court" (2.1.59) who, surfeited with pleasures, ignore those who suffer.

> "'Tis right," quoth he, "thus misery doth part
> The flux of company." Anon a careless herd,
> Full of the pasture, jumps along by him
> And never stays to greet him. "Ay," quoth Jaques,
> "Sweep on, you fat and greasy citizens,
> 'Tis just the fashion. Wherefore do you look
> Upon that poor and broken bankrupt there?"
>
> (2.1.51–57)

A notable recent article focusing on this scene is Winfried Schleiner's "Jaques and the Melancholy Stag" (175–79). Schleiner emphasizes the iconographic links between Jaques's melancholy and the stag. He points to an old tradition that associates the stag with coldness and dryness, two characteristics of the melancholic, and observes that medical treatises of the seventeenth century frequently indicate the medicinal value of the tear of the hart. The following sixteenth century account by Scaliger turns up with some variation in later medical treatises:

> We consider very highly in our treasures of the muses the tear of the stag, a matter perhaps less known to you. Before its hundreth year there isn't any [tear] in the stag. After that age it grows at the orb of the eye, from the bones themselves and bulging out stiffens into bone of a hardness surpassing horn. Where it stands out, it is round, of the outstanding brightness of deep yellow, not without traces of darker little veins. It is of such lightness that hardly touched, it escapes: it withdraws in such a way that it almost seems to move itself.[5]

Known as *lapis bezoar*, the hart's tear was considered a specific cure for melancholy. Just how the tear hardened is left mysterious, but in light of belief in its curative properties, Schleiner comments that "the stag with 'big round teares' coursing 'one another down his innocent nose in piteous chase,' a scene 'much marked of the melancholy Jaques' also perhaps generates and holds out the panacea" (177). I agree, and add that it is significant Jaques fails to take this available cure.

SOLITUDE

Behind Jaques's disdain for the greasy citizens who, surfeited with the pleasures of the pasture, cannot be bothered by a sufferer, is a residue of the renunciation of worldly things that accompanies religious solitude. Jaques has withdrawn to the forest and abandoned the life of the court in a way that suggests the religious hermit's withdrawal to the desert. His action, however, is devoid of spiritual meaning, inasmuch as Jaques neither meditates nor studies. Reclining beneath the ancient oak, Jaques embodies the worst of what empty solitude can offer. He has become so obsessed with self that he believes his misfortunes mark him off from other men as unique. The Duke's comment—perhaps the shrewdest observation in the play—suggests that Jaques needs to be disabused of his role as solitary: "I think he be transform'd into a beast,/For I can no where find him like a man" (2.7.1–2). The desire for solitude and predilection for withdrawal to sequestered, even dark, places is a common symptom of melancholy; as Du Laurens comments, "Melancholike men are also enemies to the Sunne, and shunne the light, because their spirits and humours are altogether contrary to the light" (*Discourse*, 96).

Isolation from society is never presented as a positive good by Shakespeare; for him the cloistered life is unnatural. Theseus's portrait of the solitary life of a nun, for instance, is meant to frighten Hermia in *A Midsummer's Night's Dream*,

> For aye to be in a shady cloister mew'd,
> To live a barren sister all your life,

Chaunting faint hymns to the cold fruitless moon.
Thrice blessed they that master so their blood
To undergo such maiden pilgrimage;
But earthlier happy is the rose distill'd,
Than that which withering on the virgin thorn
Grows, lives, and dies in single blessedness.

(1.1.71–78)

Regarding community a nuisance, alienated from the other inhabitants of the forest, Jaques is bound to chant anthems "to the cold fruitless moon." His desire for isolation, his wish, as he tells Orlando, that they "meet as little as we can" (3.2.257) is the opposite of the active love which Celia practices "which teacheth . . . that thou and I am one" (1.2.97).

Pastoral life had its pitfalls, as those who attempted to lead contemplative lives well knew. Rightly used, withdrawal leads to thought, reading and writing; misused, to vanity and idleness or, more properly, *acedia*. In his scholarly study of *acedia*, Siegfried Wenzel warns against the tendency to view the history of *acedia* in the later Middle Ages "as a linear change of meaning from spiritual dryness or inappetence to plain laziness" (165). But he does stress that the fate of the sin was a sort of secularization, causing it to pass from "a 'vice of the spirit' to a 'vice of the flesh'" (Wenzel, 165). Wenzel clarifies the classification of *acedia* as a carnal or a spiritual vice, citing two passages by the late thirteenth century theologian John of Wales. In his *Summa justitiae*, John writes: "According to other authorities, *acedia* is sadness or tedium against spiritual good, which we owe God."[6] But previously he had classified *acedia* as a carnal vice because of its relationship to bodily needs:

. . . we now treat of the remaining three [vices] by which the outer man is deformed and disordered, viz., *acedia*, gluttony, and lust. For *acedia* seems partially to belong to the body. Chrysostom, in *hom. imperf.* 18, says there are chiefly three natural passions which are proper to the flesh: first, eating and drinking; second, a man's love for a woman; and third, sleep.[7]

Thus, one of the two sides of *acedia* derives from the natural need to sleep. A near contemporary of John of Wales, David of Augsburg, adds to the term's complexity by distinguishing not two but *three* types of *acedia*: "torpor of [or] laziness" in performing spiritual duties, "boredom with things that belong to God" and "bitterness of mind," thus tying the vice to the melancholy humour and tending to secularize the theological vice.[8] David's description of *acedia* is one of five Wenzel cited, explicitly, relating the vice to the melancholic humour, thus bringing the concept of *acedia* closer to the medical tradition. Augsburg relates the signs of *acedia* to mental conditions that, in one seeking or intending to seek spirituality, can involve the mechanisms of melancholy:

> The vice of *accidia* has three kinds. The first is a certain bitterness of the mind which cannot be pleased by anything cheerful or wholesome. It feeds upon disgust and loathes human intercourse. This is what the Apostle [Paul?] calls the sorrow of the world that worketh death. It inclines to despair, diffidence, and suspicions, and sometimes drives its victim to suicide when he is oppressed by unreasonable grief. Such sorrow arises sometimes from previous impatience, sometimes from the fact that one's desire for some object has been delayed or frustrated, and sometimes from the abundance of melancholic humors, in which case it behooves the physician rather than the priest to prescribe a remedy.[9]

From this description one can see how natural it was to see in "the sin" grief or disease rather than spiritual inertia. Wenzel, nonetheless, emphasizes that the "survival of medieval *acedia* in Renaissance melancholy is ... a hypothetical development which cannot be demonstrated to have happened in the same way as a plant grows or a chemical change takes place" (186). The melancholy Jaques is certainly no ascetic. His life of rustic solitude is more inclined to self-involved reverie than contemplation or study. While from this negative perspective the concept of *acedia* may shed some light on Jaques's nature, melancholy in general seems more related to his sense of isolation and need for withdrawal.

TIME

Central both to the play and the question of melancholy is *time* and a related theme, *exclusion from love*. The implication of Jaques's famous seven-ages of man speech (2.7.139–66) is that human life is without meaning or purpose, an unreal theatrical performance wherein "all the men and women" are "merely players" with "their exits and their entrances." Not only does Jaques protract the melancholy saturnine period over the last two ages, but even the early stages are marked by a sour view of the world, with the infant "mewling and puking," the schoolboy "whining," the lover "sighing . . . a woeful ballad," the soldier "seeking the bubble reputation," and so on, into the emptiness of oblivion. In Jaques's jaundiced view, the seven-act play of life is pointless and absurd. It leads, furthermore, to the obliteration of life since, as William Shaw has noted, Jaques's rendering of the traditional seven-ages paradigm leaves out the sun, "the source of energy and life itself" (28). The significance of Jaques's omitting the solar age and replacing it with the Martian (associated with the "soldier") cannot be overemphasized, for Shakespeare recognized the sun's importance in maintaining a healthy balance among the various influences of the planets, so crucial to human temperament as understood in humoural theory:

> And therefore is the glorious planet Sol
> In noble eminence enthron'd and spher'd
> Amidst the other; whose med'cinable eye
> Corrects the [ill aspects] of [planets evil]
> (*Troilus and Cressida* 1.3.89–92)

In terms of the astrological paradigm, replacing the medicinal "planet Sol" with Mars in Jaques's speech allows Saturn's melancholy influence to go unchecked. For that reason the passage culminates in two protracted descriptions of the stages of old age and final senility:

> The sixth age shifts
> Into the lean and slipper'd pantaloon,
> With spectacles on nose, and pouch on side,
> His youthful hose, well sav'd, a world too wide
> For his shrunk shank, and his big manly voice,
> Turning again toward childish treble, pipes
> And whistles in his sound. Last scene of all,
> That ends this strange eventful history,
> Is second childishness, and mere oblivion,
> Sans teeth, sans eyes, sans taste, sans everything.
>
> (2.7.157–66)

The sad prospect of extended old age and protracted deterioration fits well Jaques's joyless, melancholy view of everything.

The pastoral world of the Forest of Arden ought, of course, to be oblivious to time, but as David Young points out, "there can scarcely be another play in which the characters are so time conscious" (59). Touchstone, the fool-critic with whom Jaques shares place as critical observer in the play, no sooner utters his first words to Jaques then he turns to his "dial" with "lack-lustre eye" (2.7.20–21). Touchstone's speech, which Jaques recounts some 117 lines before his own, both anticipates and mocks it:

> "It is ten a clock.
> Thus we may see," quoth he, "how the world wags.
> 'Tis but an hour ago since it was nine,
> And after one hour more 'twill be eleven,
> And so from hour to hour, we ripe and ripe,
> And then, from hour to hour, we rot and rot."
>
> (2.7.22–27)

Their fellow characters are constantly asking the time,

complaining about lateness, or carping about how in this life we not only live out the "strange, eventful history" of seven ages but ripe and rot from hour to hour. It is quite pointless for Orlando, the lover who is late for his appointments, to point out that "there's no clock in the forest" (3.2.301–02).

In his article, "Time in *As You Like It*," Jay Halio observes that Rosalind's perception of time, "however related to the preoccupation imported from the 'outside' world, is different from Touchstone's obsession with 'riping and rotting.' It is partly, the awareness of a girl in love" (204). The lover's view of time is individual and has nothing in common with the sour destiny portrayed for man in Jaques's speech. To the eager Rosalind, anxious to see her lover, Orlando's excuse for his lateness— "I come within an hour" (4.1.42)—is weak: to a woman in love an hour has no meaning, and might as well be an eternity:

> *Rosalind.* Break an hour's promise in love! He
> that will divide a minute into a thousand parts,
> and break but a part of the thousand part of a
> minute in the affairs of love, it may be said of him
> that Cupid hath clapp'd him o' th' shoulder.
>
> (4.1.44–48)

Though in matters of love Rosalind displays, as Halio well notes, a "perfectly human-romantic bias" (206), she balances this bias with realism, as one can see in her witty view of time before and after marriage: "men are April when they woo, December when they wed; maids are May when they are maids, but the sky changes when they are wives" (4.1.147–49). Rosalind's sense of time becomes, at the play's end, a compromise between the timeless forest and the hectic court. Her view of the role of time in human life is at once serious, witty, and light—not only different from Jaques's perverse perspective, but from that of Shakespeare's Troilus as well, who saw time as a dark force of separation controlling the destiny of lovers. "Time travels in divers paces with divers persons," Rosalind says to Orlando in act 3,

> I'll tell you who Time ambles withal, who Time
> trots withal, who Time gallops withal, and who he
> stands still withal.
>
> (3.2.308–11)

Citing this passage, Robert B. Bennett has sagely commented that "by defining time in relation to persons rather than persons in relation to time, she comically but accurately establishes human nature's capacity to govern time" (197).

The conquest of time is suggested at the play's end in the marriage of four couples. Human life may be "but a flower" (5.3.28), mortality obvious in the fact that "men have died, from time to time, and worms have eaten them" (4.1.92–94), and the pervasive pessimism of Jaques's account of the ages of man leads to the grave; nonethess, no other comedy by Shakespeare culminates in the wedding of so many couples: "Here's eight that must take hands/To join in Hymen's bands" (5.4.128–29). Implicit in the circle of dancing couples is the establishment of a new society that will flow from the future progeny of the newly married:

> Wedding is great Juno's crown,
> O blessed bond of board and bed!
> 'Tis Hymen peoples every town,
>
> (5.4.141–43)

Exclusion from Love

In matters of love Jaques is an outsider, except when he engages a woebegone lover in conversation so that he may be one of love's critics, as in this dialogue with Orlando:

> *Jaques.* The worst fault you have is to be in love.
> *Orlando.* 'Tis a fault I will not change for your best
> virtue. I am weary of you.

Jaques. By my troth, I was seeking for a fool when I found you.
Orlando. He is drown'd in the brook; look but in, and you shall see him.
Jaques. There I shall see mine own figure.
Orlando. Which I take to be either a fool or a cipher.
Jaques. I'll tarry no longer with you. Farewell, good Signior Love.
Orlando. I am glad of your departure. Adieu, good Monsieur Melancholy.

(3.2.282–94)

This is one of the rare occasions in the play when Orlando is given the opportunity to have the last word in a wit-parry; Jaques, as love's eccentric enemy, is an easy mark. For the most part, Orlando, along with Silvius and Phoebe, provokes amusement in the play by letting the perils of courtship cast him into the love melancholy Shakespeare was so fond of portraying in the romantic comedies and even in the early tragedy, *Romeo and Juliet* (act 1 finds the pre-Juliet Romeo lovesick over Rosaline).

In a more representative dialogue with Orlando, Rosalind gets the better of him when she ridicules Orlando for saying that he will die if he does not win the object of his love. She tries to prove that during 6,000 years no man ever died for love, citing first Troilus, who "had his brains dash'd out with a Grecian club, yet he did what he could to die before" (4.1.100–02).[10] Rosalind concludes "men have died from time to time and worms have eaten them but not for love." (4.1.97–99). In fact, however, from the medical perspective, she is wrong. In *Mystical Bedlam*, Michael MacDonald, drawing on notes of case histories compiled by the seventeenth century physician, Richard Napier, documents many instances demonstrating that "men (and women too) did die for love" (90). And earlier medical treatises are full of references to patients who suffer from love melancholy and die at their own hands, or at the hands of a physician who engages in too much bloodletting or other ill treatment. But

Rosalind, and probably Shakespeare, stand with the skeptics. If not one of love's eccentrics, like Jaques, Shakespeare was very likely one of love's realists, who might have thought along the practical lines of his own Henry V: "before God, Kate, I cannot look greenly, nor gasp out my eloquence, . . . If thou canst love me . . . take me! if not, to say to thee that I shall die, is true; but for thy love, by the Lord, no; yet I love thee too" (*Henry V* 5.2.142–52).

King Henry's position is far more open, however, than Jaques's final stand on love: Jaques will be accepting, even generous, to lovers, but resolutely a loner himself. His dignified exit at the end of *As You Like It* amounts to a protracted "no thanks, I'll pass":

> (*To Orlando*) You to a love, that your true faith doth merit;
> (*Oliver*) You to your land, and love, and great allies;
> (*To Silvius*) You to a long and well-deserved bed;
> (*To Touchstone*) And you to wrangling, for thy loving voyage
> Is but for two months victuall'd.—So, to your pleasures,
> I am for other than dancing measures.
>
> (5.4.186–93)

This speech is important to our understanding of Jaques as he is by the final scene of the play. In *A Natural Perspective*, Northrop Frye observes that Jaques is "simply opposed by temperament to festivity" and that he symbolizes "a hidden world" (100). Frye does not spell out what that "hidden world" might signify, but clearly it is tied to Jaques's isolation and renders him antithetical to the wedding celebration. William P. Shaw sees Jaques's choice of isolation as an "aberration." As he comments, "In Shakespeare's plays, isolation from society is not a natural condition of life; it is a condition Shakespeare's comic villains and tragic figures usually *suffer*, not choose" (27). Shaw concludes, therefore, that Jaques's choice of exile is "the crowning expression of his egocentricity" (28) and not a choice that is spiritually based:

Jaques has rejected the organic perspective and embraced its antithesis—one which precludes growth, interdependency in community, toleration, equilibrium, purpose, joy and love, or any prospect for renewal. Rather than dance to the rhythms of life "with measures heaped in joy," Jaques opts out: "I am other than for dancing measures" (29).

Jaques, then, can be seen as providing a minority perspective on the happiness of the wedding celebrants. That Shakespeare's emphasis is on that, there can be no doubt from the moment the Duke calls out for music and urges the couples to begin dancing: "you brides and bridegrooms all,/With measure heap'd in joy, to th' measures fall." (5.4.178–79). The staging of this final scene usually helps strike a bold note of joy. However, Canada's Stratford Company, in its summer 1983 production, took an interesting approach in staging the concluding wedding dance. Adam, the old, faithful, solitary servant who represents the virtues of the antique world, was placed at the center of the circle of wedded couples amidst torches and greenery. The death of old Adam is inevitable. Still, he is made part of the concluding ring of dancers in a way that visually demonstrates art conquering death and love triumphing over isolation. At the play's end, Jaques has turned away from the pleasures offered by court life and marriage to devote himself to solitary intellectual pleasures.

Seen as a whole, of course, *As You Like It* examines the abuses that typically go along with melancholy—those involving love and those involving contemplation. At the play's end, Jaques takes no part in the dance, because he cannot. He may, however, deserve more his self-appointed role as observer-critic, inasmuch as he has developed to the point where he can talk and listen to love's servants. Thus, even though Jaques rejects the community of love, he appears more able to advance in individual wisdom. If Francis Bacon is correct in his notion that "in this theatre of man's life it is reserved only for god and angels to be lookers-on," then, by the play's conclusion, Jaques is closer to being one of the angels. The absence of a real integration of mind and body in Jaques may recall the near-psychological schism of Chaucer's Troilus who, on the one hand, found heaven in the embraces of Criseyde, and, on the other, ended in the eighth sphere speaking the language of Dante's St. Bernard in prayer to Mary. The need for reintegrating the realms of the spiritual and the earthly, of the mind and body, of reality and imagination, is a problem Shakespeare handles more complexly in *Hamlet*.

TRAVEL

The theme of travel is linked to the melancholy Jaques almost as closely as his exclusion from love; moreover, travel has its associations with medical thinking on melancholy. Most obviously, taking a trip was thought therapeutic well into the nineteenth century: Claudius, for example, sends Hamlet to England, and variation 13 of Elgar's *Enigma Variations* ties sea voyage to recovery from unhappy romantic love. As Du Laurens observes in his *Discourse*, "Remouing, that is to say, the chaunging of the ayre, is on of the rarest remedies" (123). But in Jaques's case, travel seems to be at least the partial cause of the malady. By his own account, his melancholy owes something to "the sundry contemplation of my travels, in which [my] often rumination wraps me in a most humorous sadness" (4.1.17–20). Rosalind also appears to attribute the cause of Jaques's melancholy to his extensive traveling:

> Farewell, Monsieur Traveller: look you lisp and wear
> strange suits; disable all the benefits of your own country;
> be out of love with your nativity, and almost chide God for
> making you that countenance you are; or I will scarce think
> you have swam in a gundello.
>
> (4.1.33–38)

Ennui and scorn had, by the time Shakespeare wrote *As*

You Like It, become traditional character traits for the traveler, returned home, who found life in England barbarous by comparison to the sophistication of the continent. Marston's *Second Satire*, written about 1578, for example, contains this description of the unhappy traveler, Bruto, upon his return to England from the continent:

> "Look, look, with what a discontented grace
> Bruto the traveller doth sadly pace
> 'Long Westminster! O civil-seeming shade,
> Mark his sad colours!—how demurely clad!
> Staidness itself, and Nestor's gravity,
> Are but the shade of his civility.
> And now he sighs.
>
> (*Works* 3.274.127–33)

A similar example of a melancholic traveler, disappointed with home, appears in Thomas Nashe's *Pierce Penilesse* (1592):

> All *Italionato* is his talke, & his spade peak is as sharpe as if he had been a Pioner before the walls of *Room*. . . . If he be challenged to fight, for his delatorye excuse, hee obiects that it is not the custome of the Spaniard or the Germaine, to looke back to euery dog that barkes. (Works, 168–69)

On the score of appearing to Rosalind as "Monsieur Traveller," Jaques cuts a figure that probably has as much to do with Shakespeare's knowledge of the literary conventions of his age as the aspects of melancholia detailed in the medical prose writing. The melancholy traveler, indeed, even has an earlier permutation in Shakespeare's own Don Adriano de Armado, "a refined traveller of Spain,/A man in all the world's new fashion planted/That hath a mint of phrases in his brain" (*Love's Labor's Lost*, 1.1.163–65). Like Armado, Jaques fancies himself a clever wit, for which reason the members of the court welcome him in Arden for their amusement. One peripheral association of melancholy and travel is, of course, the presumption that the continent will have tempted the traveler into sexual indulgence, which, in turn, frequently led to dejected spirits or worse. Burton's *Anatomy of Melancholy* speaks to this point (1.333), but it, of course, was published in 1621, after Shakespeare's death. The idea, however, was common in the playwright's own day. We find in Marston, for instance;

> Sad, Bruto, say,
> Art anything but only sad array?
> Which I am sure is all thou brought'st from France,[11]

and in Robert Greene, who complains in *The Repentance of Robert Green* (1592) that fellow students at Cambridge led him "to trauell into Italy, and Spaine, in which places I sawe and practizde such villainie as is abhominable to declare" (*The Bodley Head Quartos*, 6:19–20). Duke Senior's attack on Jaques's libertinism in which he speaks of the railer as "sensual as the brutish sting itself" and as covered with "embossed sores, and headed evils,/that thou with license of free foot has caught" (2.7.66–68) certainly draws on this commonplace.

The Duke's attack on the melancholy, cynical traveler, moreover, lends emphasis to the angry malcontent dimension of Jaques's character as it is presented in this early scene. Duke Senior's retort is a direct response to Jaques's expressed desire to play the curative role of the satirist:

>   give me leave
> To speak my mind, and I will through and through
> Cleanse the foul body of th' infected world,
> If they will patiently receive my medicine.
>
>   (2.7.58–61)

Duke Senior is merely observing that Jaques's own flaws make him ineligible to cast stones. Jaques's defense against the Duke's charges adds even more weight to the view that Jaques is a melancholic man of the choleric, cynical variety. He questions what man is free of the taint of corruption?

What woman in the city do I name,
When that I say the city-woman bears
The cost of princes on unworthy shoulders?
Who can come in and say that I mean her,
When such a one as she, such is her neighbor?
Or what is he of basest function,
That says his bravery is not on my cost,
Thinking that I mean him, but therein suits
His folly to the mettle of my speech?
There then! how then? what then? Let me see wherein
My tongue hath wronged him.

(2.7.74–84)

Such a view of the world would make for a very dark play, indeed, except for the fact that Jaques appears in a comedy and much of the time we are laughing at him. Laughter undercuts his credibility and force as a critical commentator.

In *As You Like It*, we find Shakespeare treating melancholy with grace, a light touch, even humour; however, when he arrives at *Hamlet*, perhaps the greatest tragedy of his mature period, Shakespeare's portrait of melancholy is transformed into one of massive proportions.

FIVE

Hamlet

Shakespeare, Melancholy and the Renaissance Physicians

Shakespeare's knowledge of Elizabethan humoural theory was thorough, as the doctor's remark in the introduction to *The Taming of the Shrew* makes clear: "melancholy is the nurse of frenzy" (*Induction* 2.133). Like Chaucer, who, describing the sorrows of Arcite in *The Knight's Tale*, characterized his behavior as "lyk manye/Engendred of humour malencolik" (1374–75), Shakespeare possessed a rather sophisticated understanding of the relationship between melancholy and mania. It appears again, for example, in *Hamlet* when the Prince ridicules Gertrude's idea that the ghost he sees is due to "ecstacy":

[Ecstasy!]
My pulse as yours doth temperately keep time,
And makes as healthful music.

(3.4.139–41)

One of the symptoms of mania is the quickening of the heart and pulse rate. If Hamlet's mother fears that her son—who for three acts has been feeling dejected and melancholy—is seeing things because of the "ecstacy" of mania, she is taking for granted an association between melancholic and manic conditions. The assumption that the two are related is, indeed, centuries old, though the idea that a cyclic disorder is involved is relatively new.

Scholars of a generation or two ago, among them, Levin Schücking, Murray Bundy, Ruth Anderson, A. C. Bradley, John Dover Wilson and, more recently, Bridget Lyons, have discussed Hamlet as a preeminent representative of the melancholy type as the Elizabethans understood it. But only with the close scrutiny of medical treatises of the time, such as we have in Mary I. O'Sullivan's examination of Shakespeare and Timothy Bright's *Treatise of Melancholy*, do we begin to see the strong parallels between Shakespeare's perceptions of melancholic behavior and those of Renaissance physicians (667–79).

Schücking regards Hamlet as a melancholic type, as it is described in the character books "so beloved of the Elizabethans" (27). Bundy views Hamlet as a character suffering "a basic lack of equilibrium" (540) whose "downfall is brought about by the subjection of all the will to the lower souls, to passion, appetite, and imagination" (549). For him the hero presents a moral rather than a medical problem. Though Anderson is not primarily concerned with *Hamlet*, she says of the medical treatises, "since we have found that Shakespeare was conversant with their theories, it is possible that he drew them from here" (163). Bradley cites no sixteenth century medical writers, makes one reference in passing to Robert Burton, yet considers Hamlet's melancholy "the centre of the tragedy" (107). Bradley's confusion about the boundaries of the disease "melancholy" is evident in the fact that he considers "Hamlet's condition may truly be called diseased" if melancholy explains his failure to act, and yet he must conclude that "this melancholy is something very different from insanity" (103). Even the experts have trouble deciding where sadness and mopishness leave off and the disease begins. Wilson's *What Happens in Hamlet* is a thoughtful rethinking of the play as performance that, while including O'Sullivan's findings on Bright and adding some new ones of his own in an appendix, is not primarily concerned with the question of melancholy (309–20). In her study of *Hamlet* in *Voices of Melancholy*, Lyons focuses on "the literary possibilities that melancholy provided" but makes her consideration of the medical writing minimal (15).

I propose to demonstrate that Shakespeare depicts Hamlet as a sufferer of melancholic *disease* (not melancholy *temperament*) as it is generally understood by such representative Renaissance physicians as Timothy Bright, André du Laurens, Andrew Boorde, Juan Huarte de San Juan and Levinius Lemnius. I shall also claim that Du Laurens was more influential on Shakespeare's writing than anyone has so far suggested.

While my basic assumption is that the continuity of Elizabethan views about melancholy (as they appear in works by Shakespeare and his medical contemporaries) is part of the continuity of Elizabethan culture generally, this is not to say Shakespeare "lifted" the symptomatology of melancholy found in various Renaissance medical writers to design Hamlet's character in a systematic one-to-one sort of way. Modern psychiatrists and psychoanalysts have seen Hamlet's disease in terms of manic-depressive psychosis and the unresolved Oedipus complex—a later and rather different story providing yet another body of thought that may help to understand the play's genesis and that, for some critics, offers an approach to analysis of the text. To some extent, Shakespeare the playwright anticipates the direction taken by modern psychoanalysis; for this reason it is unsurprising that those of a Freudian persuasion have found *Hamlet* useful. Jacques Lacan sounds almost ingenuous, in a seminar conducted in 1959, observing—"I know of no commentator who has ever taken the trouble to make this remark . . . from one end of *Hamlet* to the other, all anyone talks about is mourning" (39). Arthur Kirsch, whose 1981 *Journal of English Literary History* article, "Hamlet's Grief," is included in Harold Bloom's 1990 collection of essays on the play, stands essentially with Lacan (that is, with Sigmund Freud) as he underscores his thesis: "grief composes its essential emotional content" (122).

I am not, however, primarily concerned with the Shakespeare who anticipates the discoveries of later science. I want, rather, to undertake the kind of study of Shakespeare's portrait of melancholy that will reveal a relationship between Shakespeare and an area of Renaissance medicine truly representing a "dynamic exchange," in the sense that Stephen Greenblatt uses the term in his recent book, *Shakespearean Negotiations* (11). The first chapter of that book, "The Circulation of Social Energy," contains a number of abjurations about what Greenblatt calls the "energy" contained in the various areas of Renaissance culture, one of which is "there can be no appeals to genius as the sole origin of the energies of great art" (12). I agree, and where Shakespeare's "exchanges" with the Renaissance medical world yield reflections or parallels in his delineations of melancholy, it is especially easy to comply. Where, however, we find instances of Shakespeare the playwright striking out ahead of the scientists of his own time, heading off even Freud and later twentieth century psychiatrists, some reservation must be added. Shakespeare's "exchanges" from time to time so outweigh what he was given that it is harder not to invoke the term "genius."

HAMLET, GRIEF AND THE GHOST

In his introduction to the Facsimile Text Society's edition of Timothy Bright's *A Treatise of Melancholie*, Hardin Craig writes,

> Shakespeare may have known Bright's *Treatise of Melancholie*. It was available, simple, and authoritative. The stock of Thomas Vautrollier passed into the hands of Richard Field, Shakespeare's fellow townsman and the publisher of *Venus and Adonis* and *The Rape of Lucrece*. The accurate description of melancholic symptoms in *Hamlet* and other plays reminds one of Bright. In *Hamlet* and in the sonnets there are a number of fairly close verbal echoes. But the question is not easily solved, since a good deal of the phraseology is current medical language and since the knowledge which Shakespeare possessed was also available in a number of other works. (Craig, xvi)

Bright began his career as a physician and ended it as a clergyman. He took his M.B. at Cambridge in 1573–74, became a licentiate in medicine in 1575, and a doctor of medicine in 1578–79 (Keynes, 3). He died vicar of St. Mary's, Shrewsbury, and, as has often been pointed out, there are signs of both lives in his *Treatise of Melancholie*, which presents spiritual consolation together with principles of psychology (see, for example, O'Sullivan, 668). In fact, Bright will not only give spiritual consolation but "advise of physicke help" as well (iiii). In 1585 Timothy Bright was made resident physician of St. Bartholomew's Hospital. There in May 1586 he wrote the dedication to the *Treatise*, first printed in that year by Thomas Vautrollier of Blackfriars. It became popular enough for three editions, two in 1586 and a third in 1613.

The first scholar to suggest that Shakespeare had read Bright was an anonymous contributor to *Notes and Queries* in 1853 (7:546) who observed that Hamlet's phrase, "discourse of reason" (1.2.150), also appears in the dedicatory epistle to the *Treatise*:

> I haue enterlaced my treatise besides with disputes of
> Philosophie that the learned sort of them, and such as
> are of quicke conceit, and delited in discourse of reason
> in naturall things, may find to passe their time with.
> (Bright, iiii)

Later, in *Shakspere and Typography*, William Blades pro-
posed that Shakespeare at the start of his London career
had been a press reader or shop assistant to Vautrollier,
to whom he may have been introduced by Richard Field,
Vautrollier's apprentice and successor as well as Shakespeare's neighbor in Stratford (Keynes, 9). Wilson is correct, I think, in labelling Blade's observation a *lucky
shot*: "It would be an interesting task to compare the
Mad Folk of Shakespeare, most of whom have the melancholy fit, with *A Treatise of Melancholie*, which was
probably read carefully for press by the youthful poet"
(Wilson, 310). Wilson and O'Sullivan give most weight to
earlier scholars, Richard Loening, who asserted that
Bright was "the source of Shakespeare's psychology both
in *Hamlet* and other plays,"[1] and Dowden, who stated in
a note (on 2.2.10) that "I can hardly doubt that Shakespeare was acquainted with Bright's *Treatise*."[2]

Both Wilson and O'Sullivan have independently culled
an exhaustive string of parallels between the *Treatise* and
Shakespeare's works. Among those Wilson (dealing only
with *Hamlet*) and O'Sullivan found are four most striking ones:

1. In chapter 4 of this *Treatise*, Bright speaks of "the
braine as tender as a posset curd" (13), and in chapter 11,
The cure by medicine, meete for melancholie persons,
Bright observes in a technical passage, "melancholy
blood is thicke and grosse, & therfore easily floweth not
though the vaine be opened" (270) and then explains
remedies for thinning the blood and obtaining an easier
flow. This may be compared to the Ghost's words to
Hamlet, significant as verbal borrowing or an adaptation
of sorts:

Sleeping within my orchard,
My custom always of the afternoon,
Upon my secure hour thy uncle stole,
With juice of cursed hebona in a vial,
And in the porches of my ears did pour
The leprous distillment, whose effect
Holds such an enmity with blood of man
That swift as quicksilver it courses through
The natural gates and alleys of the body,
And with a sudden vigor it doth [posset]
And curd, like eager droppings into milk,
the thin and wholesome blood.

(1.5.59–70)

2. In a discussion of *How melancholicke persons are to order themselues in the rest of their diet, and what choise they are to make of ayre, meate, and drinke, house, and apparell* (chapter 39), Bright states, "the ayre meet for melancholicke folke ought to be thinne, pure, and subtile, open and patent to all winds: in respect of their temper, especially to the South and Southeast." A most convincing parallel occurs in Hamlet's words to Guildenstern, "I am but mad north-northwest. When the wind is southerly I know a hawk from a handsaw" (2.2.378–79).

3. Bright seems almost to summarize the mood shifts of Hamlet's antic dispostion in chapter 17, *How melancholy procureth feare, sadnes, dispaire, and such other passions:*

> The perturbations of melancholy are for the most parte, sadde and fearefull, and such as rise of them: as distrust, doubt, diffidence, or dispaire, sometimes furious, and sometimes merry in apparaunce, through a kinde of Sardonian, and false laughter, as the humour, is disposed that procureth these diversities. (102)

Compare Hamlet's words to Horatio, in the ghost scene wherein he announces that he will assume the role of melancholic madman:

Here, as before, never so help you mercy,
How strange or odd some'er I bear myself—
As I perchance hereafter shall think meet
To put an antic dispostion on—
That you, at such times seeing me, never shall,
With arms encumb'red thus, or this headshake,
Or by pronouncing of some doubtful phrase,
As "Well, well, we know," or "We could and if we would,"
Or "If we list to speak," or "there be, and if they might,"
Or such ambiguous giving out, to note
That you know aught of me—. . . ."

(1.5.169–79)

4. In chapter 38, *How melancholicke persons are to order themselues in their affections*, Bright uses comparisons to music that seem to reappear more simply in Ophelia's words in act 3:

> This effect is wrought by that kinde of disorder, in the like manner, a perturbation whereon reason sitteth not, and holdeth not the raine, is of the same aptness to disturbe the goodly order, disposed by iust proportion in our bodies: & putting the parts of that most consonant, & pleasant harmony out of tune deliuer a note, to the great discontentment of reason, and much against the mindes will, which intendeth far other, then the coporall instrument effecteth. (*Treatise*, 250–51)

>   Oh, what a noble mind is here o'erthrown!
> The courtier's, soldier's, scholar's, eye, tongue, sword,
> Th' expectation and rose of the fair state,
> The glass of fashion and the mould of form,
> Th' observ'd of all observers, quite, quite, down!
> And I, of ladies most deject and wretched,
> That suck'd the honey of his [music] vows,
> Now see [that] noble and most sovereign reason
> Like sweet bells jangled, out of time, and harsh

(3.1.150–58)

O'Sullivan has also demonstrated that Shakespeare's use of Bright's *Treatise* extended beyond verbal parallels to the employment of similar ideas; notably, the doctor's many references to the connection between melancholy and procrastination may have contributed to Shakespeare's portrayal of Hamlet's delay in revenge.[3] Though she may be correct in stating that Bright's work "affected the Elizabethan imagination much as popularized theories of endocrinology, or the subconscious have affected our generation" (O'Sullivan, 668), the *Treatise* never became as well known as the studies on melancholy by Burton or Du Laurens (Jackson, *Melancholia And Depression*, 83).

André Du Laurens's *A Discourse of the Preservation of the Sight*, translated into English by Richard Surphlet (1599), contained as "the seconde Discourse" a work entitled *Melancholie Diseases and . . . the Meanes to Cure Them*. It has been judged "as authoritative in its day . . . representative of Renaissance medical thought on melancholia . . . and even a principal source for Burton in the following century" (Jackson, *Melancholia and Depression*, 86–87). The work went through many editions, and Irving I. Edgar has observed that Burton cites Du Laurens "over sixty times" (69).

Quite apart from considerations of the play's mature style, the detectable echoes of Du Laurens in Shakespeare's *Hamlet* help place the play as we know it *after* 1599, the publication date of the Du Laurens treatise. Thus a welcome byproduct of the evidence of influence from the medical text is to help distinguish Shakespeare's from the other *Hamlet* play referred to by Henslowe and Lodge. References in Henslowe's *Diary* and Thomas Lodge's *Wit's Misery* indicate there was a play called *Hamlet* in production between 1594 and 1596,[4] but it cannot have been Shakespeare's play as we have it. There are many parallel views of melancholy between Shakespeare's *Hamlet* and the Du Laurens work, but I would like to begin by pointing to a striking contrast, with which the physician opens his *Discourse* that finds an echo in the well-known prose speech of Hamlet in act 2, scene 2 ("I have of late—"). Du Laurens begins his study of melancholy with a chapter entitled *That man is a diuine and politike creature, endued with three seuerall noble powers, as Imagination, Reason and Memorie* (fol. 72). Set beside this is chapter 2—*That this living creature . . . is now and then . . . abassed and corrupted* (fol. 82), containing an ample description of the characteristics of the melancholy man. Between them these two chapters hold all the dark and light elements also contained in the famous prose speech of act 2. First, from chapter 1 of the Du Laurens study, note these two excerpts on the subject of the nobility of man:

> Amongst the Diuines, there are some which haue called him euery maner of creature, because he hath intercourse with euery maner of creature; he hath a being, as haue the stones; life, as haue the plants; and sence or feeling as the beasts; and vnderstanding, as haue the Angels. Othersome haue honoured him, giuing him the title of vniuersall gouernour, as hauing all things vnder his empire and iurisdiction, as being he to whom euery thing yeeldeth obedience, and for whose sake the whole world was created. In brief, this is the chiefe and principall of Gods worke, and the most noble of all other creatures. (fol. 73)

> The Arabians haue so highly commended it, that they haue verely beleeued, that the minde by vertue of the imagination could worke miracles, pearce the heauens, commaunde the elements, lay plaine the huge mountaines, and make mountaines of the plaine ground. (fol. 76)

The clinical definition of melancholia in chapter 2, on the other hand, presents a contrasting picture of one of the ways things may go wrong:

> The melancholike man properly so called, (I meane him which hath the disease in the braine) is ordinarilie out of heart, . . . he would runne away and cannot goe, he goeth alwaies sighing, troubled with the hicket, and with vnseparable sadnes, which oftentimes turneth into dispayre; he is alwaies disquieted both in bodie and spirit, he is subiect to watchfulnes, which doth consume him on the one side, and vnto sleepe, which tormenteth him on the

other side . . . hee is assayled with a thousand vaine visions, and hideous buggards, with fantasticall inuentions, and dreadfull dreames;. . . . To conclude, hee is become a sauadge creature, haunting the shadowed places, suspicious solitarie, enemie to the Sunne, and one whom nothing can please, but onely discontentment, which forgeth vnto it selfe A thousand false and vaine imaginations. (fol. 82)

The words Shakespeare gives Hamlet in his second act conversations with Rosencrantz and Guildenstern seem to conflate the contrasting possibilities Du Laurens outlines in his first two chapters:

> I have of late—but wherefore I know
> not—lost all my mirth, forgone all custom of
> exercises; and indeed it goes so heavily with my
> disposition, that this goodly frame, the earth,
> seems to me a sterile promontory; this most
> excellent canopy, the air, look you, this brave
> o'erhanging firmament, this majestical roof
> fretted with golden fire, why, it appeareth no
> other thing to me than a foul and pestilent
> congregation of vapors. What[a] piece of work
> is a man, how noble in reason, how infinite in
> faculties, in form and moving, how express and
> admirable in action, how like an angel in
> apprehension, how like a god! The beauty of the
> world; the paragon of animals; and yet to me what
> is this quintessence of dust? Man delights not me.
> (2.2.295–309)

Hamlet clearly feels an apathetic indifference toward things which used to please him, and he seems to be one of those who, according to Du Laurens's symptomatology of the disease, "are weary of their lives, hate the world," "one whom nothing can please, but only discontentment." Earlier in the play Hamlet cries out,

> Oh god, God,
> How [weary], stale, flat, and unprofitable

> Seem to me all the uses of this world!
> fie on't, ah fie! 'tis an unweeded garden.
>
> (1.2.132–35)

From the outset Hamlet projects more than what the Elizabethan considered merely the melancholy complexion. In the second scene, references to the clouds still hanging on him (66), his "nighted color" (68), and his "inky cloak" (78) recall a commonplace about melancholics Du Laurens plainly states, that black is "that colour which they most loue, as being enemies to Sun and light" (fol. 90). Melancholy is often denoted by the black suits worn by scholars and artists, soldiers and statesman who appear in contemporary Renaissance portraits by Titian, Bronzino and Veronese (Frye, *The Renaissance Hamlet*, 94). Black attire frequently appears in these paintings in combination with a book placed in the scholar's hand or a sword at the soldier's side. Not melancholy alone, but deep mourning is signified by the "inky cloak" Hamlet wears amidst the general splendor of the rest of the court. When in her first words to Hamlet Gertrude urges her son to "cast thy nighted color off," she is referring to the formal funeral cloak worn as mourning attire at state funerals, which he has continued to wear in stark contrast to everyone else on stage.[5] That Hamlet is one of those who, according to Du Laurens's clinical description, "hath the disease in the braine" is further suggested in this same scene by Hamlet's response to Gertrude:

> 'Tis not alone my inky cloak, [good] mother,
> Nor customary suits of solemn black,
> Nor windy suspiration of forc'd breath,
> No, nor fruitful river in the eye,
> Nor the dejected havior of the visage,
> Together with all forms, moods, [shapes] of grief,
> That can [denote] me truly. These indeed seem,
> For they are actions that a man might play,
> But *I have that within which passeth show,*
>
> (emphasis mine; 1.2.77–85)

That last line suggests the feeling Du Laurens, in his definition, calls the "vnseparable sadness, which often-times turneth into dispayre" and leads Hamlet to thoughts of suicide: "O, that this too too sallied flesh would melt, . . .!" (1.2.129); "To die, . . . / . . . 'tis a consumma-tion/Devoutly to be wish'd" (3.1.59–63).

Ophelia's characterization of Hamlet's former qualities of courtier, soldier and scholar (3.1.151) indicates that the state of mind into which Hamlet is now sunk is the result of recent griefs. These not only lead to thoughts of suicide, but bad dreams and sleeplessness as well: "O God, I could be bounded in a nutshell, and count myself a king of infinite space—were it not that I have bad dreams" (2.2.254–56); "Sir, in my heart there was a kind of fighting/That would not let me sleep" (5.2.4–5). Ham-let's words remind one of the references in the Du Laurens description of the melancholic to "watchfulness, which doth consume" and "dreadfull dreames." In a sec-tion on dreams and the melancholic, Du Laurens recalls the Hamlet of act 3, scene 1, who longs to sleep except for the fear of the awful dreams that may come:

> HAMLET. "Tis a consummation
>   Devoutly to be wished. To die, to sleep,
>   To sleep—perchance to dream. Aye, there's the rub,
>   For in that sleep of death what dreams may come
>   When we have shuffled off this mortal coil.
>
>   (63–67)

> [Du Laurens] If at one time or other it fall out, that they be ouertaken with a little slumber, it is then but a trouble-some sleepe, accompanied with a thousand of false and fearefull apparitions, and dreames so dreadfull, as it were better for them to be awake. (fol. 95)

Later in his study the physician expands on this idea of consuming watchfulness: "melancholike folke both waking and sleeping, may be haunted with a thousand vaine inuentions" (fol. 97). Such "vaine inuentions" must be related to what Du Laurens in his long clinical description calls "false and vaine imaginations." There is evidence as early as act 1, scene 4, that Hamlet's imagination is affected in this way. When, for instance, Hamlet threatens Horatio after he tries to keep Hamlet from following the ghost to the edge of the cliff, Horatio comments to Marcellus, "He waxes desperate with [imagination]." (1.4.87). At this point in the play, while Hamlet is acting in a way that seems unreasonable, he sees what Horatio also really sees. Hamlet may be unreasonable, but his reason is not "corrupted" in the way Du Laurens would have it when he speaks of "melancholike persons [that] haue their imagination troubled" (fol. 87). In that state, vision is truly impaired. The person melancholic to that extent is blinded by the blackness of melancholy, for, as Du Laurens writes, "the minde can see nothing without the eyes" (fol. 90).

By the closet scene of act 3, scene 4, however, the overwrought imagination of Hamlet may actually have deteriorated to hallucination. Unable to see her husband's ghost herself, Gertrude's observation on her son's behavior is that Hamlet speaks "with th' incorporal air" (3.4.118) and she judges the ghost to be "the very coinage of [Hamlet's] brain" (137). At this point in the play Gertrude's conclusion indicates that, in Elizabethan terms, Hamlet's imagination is so intensely troubled that his mind cannot see. From the point of view of Du Laurens, specifically, it might be said that the reason Hamlet cannot see is that he is obsessed with his father—*not his mother*, as the Freudians conclude. Note what Du Laurens has to say about melancholia so advanced that it results in hallucination:

> *The melancholike partie may see that which is within his owne braine*, but vnder another forme, because that the spirits and blacke vapours continually passe by the sinewes, veines and arteries, from the braine vnto the ye, which causeth it to see many shadowes and untrue apparitions in the aire, whereupon from the eye the formes thereof are conveyed to vnto the imagination. (fol. 92; emphasis mine)

In the language of Freud, Hamlet sees the lost object he has incorporated, as he does the work of mourning. He sees his father.

Claudius seems fully aware of the medical implications of Hamlet's behavior even earlier in act 3:

> There's something in his soul
> O'er which his melancholy sits on brood,
>
> .   .   .   .
>
> This something-settled matter in his heart
> Whereon his brains still beating puts him thus
> From fashion of himself.
>
> (3.1.164–75)

The king's decision to send Hamlet "with speed to England" (169), is one of the common cures Du Laurens describes for melancholy: "Remouing, that is to say, the chaunging of the ayre, is on of the rarest remedies" (fol. 123).

The clinical picture of the melancholic as set forth by Du Laurens does suggest that Hamlet's behavior goes beyond the vague depression of a man like Antonio in *The Merchant of Venice*, whose sadness comes, as it were, out of thin air, and who complains quite honestly of bewilderment—"I know not why I am so sad." Hamlet knows only too well the cause of his depression. He is reacting to events so powerful they change him from the lively courtier-scholar Ophelia described into the dejected prince at the play's beginning, a trouble to both Gertrude and Claudius (for rather different reasons).

Certainly the ideas of other Renaissance physicians on the subject of melancholy helped shape Shakespeare's thinking; however, none of these seems to have had so pervasive an influence as Bright or Du Laurens, nor seems as valuable as commentary on psychological matters in contemporary terms. Du Laurens, as we have just seen, is particularly effective in his exploration of the relationship between the faculty of imagination and melancholia that is basic to the whole tradition and important to the playwright. Shakespeare not only made Hamlet fear following the ghost, lest it take advantage of his weakened imagination, and had Horatio warn his friend not to follow (1.4.69–78) for the same reason, but Shakespeare also emphasizes that for Hamlet the Gonzago play is in part a test of Hamlet's own imagination:

> If his [Claudius's] occulted guilt
> Do not itself unkennel in one speech,
> It is a damned ghost that we have seen,
> And my imaginations are as foul
> As Vulcan's stithy.
>
> (3.2.80–84)

Though not as influential, still useful in understanding *Hamlet* in Elizabethan terms are some other medical treatises of the day. The problem of corruption of the imagination in melancholics is taken up, for example, by an English monk and physician, Andrew Boorde (1490–1549), in *The Breviarie of Health*, a popular book first published in London in 1547. In his discussion of "a certen kynde of madnes named melancholia" (fol. 78r) he wrote:

> This sicknes is named the melancholy madness which is a sicknes full of fantasies, thinking to here or to see that thing that is not heard nor seene, and a man hauing this madness, shal thinke in himselfe that thing that can neuer be, for some bee so fantasticall that they will thinke themselfe God or as good, or such lyke thinges perteyning to presumption or to desperation to be dampned, the one hauing this sicknes doth not go so farre the one way, but the other doth dispayre as much the other way. (fol. 78r)

The overactive imagination of melancholic men was thought to accompany poor memory. Juan Huarte De San Juan's "Englished" *Examen de ingenios* observes that melancholics "are Weak of Memory, their own Invention is so large that their very Imagination serves them in lieu of Memory and Remembraunce" (240). This work, considered one of the first attempts to show the connection between psychology and physiology, appears to have continued to be read in the universities into the eighteenth century.[6] In *Hamlet*, when the ghost is imposing his task on his son,

> I find thee apt,
> And duller shouldst thou be than the fat weed
> That roots itself in ease on Lethe wharf,
> Wouldst thou not stir in this
>
> (1.5.32–34)

though he is primarily warning against sloth in the terms "aptness," "dullness" and "ease," his allusion to "Lethe" also reveals his concern with forgetfulness, a concern which is repeated in later warnings, "remember me" (1.2.91), "do not forget!" (3.4.110).

Among the possible causes adduced in the play for Hamlet's melancholy are those well-known in the various medical treatises. Early in the play Gertrude suggests bereavement over his father's death as a cause of Hamlet's "distemper," and somewhat later Rosencrantz and Guildenstern suppose instead frustrated ambition. Both causes are discussed by Levinius Lemnius in his *Touchstone of Complexions*,

> Some be brought into it, through long sorrow and heavynesse for the death of their Parentes, or some great losse of worldy wealth, or finally by myssing and beyng disappointed of some great desyre and expectation. (fol. 14v)

Similarly, Ophelia's account of Hamlet's appearance in her closet (2.1.74–97) gives Polonius the symptoms which lead him to the diagnosis of love melancholy, a frequently discussed subdivision of the disease in the medical literature:

> And he repell'd, a short tale to make,
> Fell into a sadness, then into a fast,
> Thence to a watch, thence into a weakness,
> Thence to [a] lightness, and by this declension

Into the madness wherein now he raves,

(2.2.146–50)

Boorde says of the lovesick that "yong persons be much troubled with this impediment" (fol. 62r) and that "This infirmitie doth come of amours which is a seruent loue, for to haue carnal copulacion with the party that is loued, and it can not be obtayned, some be so solich that they be ravished of their wittes" (fol. 62r). As a remedy Boorde advises to "muse not but use mirth and mery company, and be wise and not solich" (fol. 62v)—good advice for melancholy in general. As Bridget Lyons has pointed out vis-à-vis love melancholy, "the Ghost is even more strongly evoked by Ophelia's picture of Hamlet's pallor (cf. 1.2.232–33);" nonetheless, both Ophelia and her father misinterpret Hamlet's real reasons for melancholy (81). Even Gertrude, whose first diagnosis was a sound one—"I doubt it is no other but the main,/His father's death and our [o'erhasty] marriage" (2.2.56–57), clutches at Polonius's mistaken assessment with vain hope: "And for your part, Ophelia, I do wish/That your good beauties be the happy cause/Of Hamlet's wildnes" (3.1.38–40).

But the wicked speed with which Gertrude went from the grave of her husband to the bed of her brother-in-law is the primary problem for Hamlet: "a beast that wants discourse of reason/Would have mourn'd longer" (1.2.150–51). The problem of how love fares over time, treated lightly in As You Like It and passionately in Troilus and Cressida, here is seen in yet another light. Hamlet is outraged that his mother remarried before his father was "But two-months dead, nay, not so much, not two" (1.2.138). The intensity of Hamlet's disgust with Gertrude's behavior is unmistakable in the sarcasm of Hamlet's comment after Horatio commiserates with his friend's sense that the marriage "followed hard upon" the funeral—"Thrift, thrift, Horatio, the funeral bak'd meats/Did coldly furnish forth the marriage tables" (1.2.180–81).

One of the primary agents attempting to cure Hamlet is Claudius, at least until he becomes aware of Hamlet's murderous feelings toward himself. Before packing him off to England, he provides two friends, Rosencrantz and Guildenstern, in part, to sound out Hamlet, but also as therapy. Rosencrantz is explicit about the way he views his relationship to the Prince, "You do surely bar the door upon your own liberty if you deny your griefs to your friend" (3.2.338–39). Claudius's ostensible charge to the pair is primarily curative in motivation:

> so by your companies
> To draw him on to pleasures, and to gather
> So much as from occasion you may glean,
> Whether aught to us unknown afflicts him thus,
> That, open'd, lies within our remedy.
>
> (2.2.14–18)

Therapeutic friends are a perennial remedy for melancholy. Andrew Boorde, for example, advises "let them [melancholics] use company, & not be alone nor to muse of this thing nor of that" (fol. 78v). And Lemnius, likewise, says "exhort them to use such mery compaignyes: and often to frequent such pleasant conferences: thereby to acquainte themselues wyth curtesye & familiar humanitye" (fol. 139r).

Another less commonly discussed remedy for melancholy is the conversion of grief to anger. Two Renaissance writers who do take up the subject are the physician Bright, and the French philosopher, Pierre Charron. Bright recommends anger as a remedy only after all other avenues have failed:

> And if no other perswasion will serve a vehement passion, of another sort is to be kindled, that may withdrawe that vain and foolish sorowe into some other extremity, as of anger. . . . for although they both breed a dislike, yet that proceedeth of other cause, rebateth the force of it which first gave occasion, and as one pinne is driven out with another, so the later may expel the former. (255–56)

Along similar lines Charron writes of the violence done by suppressing anger under a pretense of calm:

> There are some that smother their choler within, to the end it breake not forth, and that they may seeme wise and moderate; but they fret themselves inwardly, and offer themselves a greater violence than the matter is worth. It is better to chide a little, and to vent the fire, to the end it be not ever-ardent and painful within . . . All diseases that appear openly are the lighter, and then are most dangerous when they rest hidden with a counterfet health. (*Of Wisdome*, 564)

In *Macbeth* Shakespeare has Malcolm give essentially this same advice more plainly to Macduff, "let grief/Convert to anger; blunt not the heart, enrage it" (4.3.228–29).

By act 3, scene 4 of *Hamlet*, the Prince has found the object of his hostility: his mother, Gertrude. Paul Jorgensen has observed of the closet scene that it "is dramatically, perhaps, the most successful in the play. . . . it is the only scene in the play in which Hamlet talking to others is as impressive as Hamlet talking to himself" (255). J. E. Hankins considers Hamlet's lashing out at his mother in this scene almost a "conversion": "Nowhere after this scene does Hamlet show the same bitterness that he had earlier expressed" (51–52). Hamlet is determined to speak daggers to Gertrude, to set the glass before her and make her conscious of her inmost soul. His "A bloody deed! almost as bad, good mother,/As kill a king, and marry with his brother" (3.4.28–29) indicates his suspicion of Gertrude's share in the murder of his father and a desire to test her reaction to his words. The alacrity with which Hamlet plunges the sword into Polonius, supposing him to be the King behind the arras, suggests his suspicions on this score are laid to rest. The manner in which Hamlet describes Gertrude's erotic pleasures and the comparison of Claudius to a "mildewed ear" (3.4.97), "a bat, a gib" (3.4.190) give expression to the sexual revulsion such ideas arouse in the Prince. While Hamlet is thus cruelly wringing his mother's heart, the ghost appears to stem the tide of Hamlet's wrath against the nearly prostrate Gertrude. Hamlet, however, is immediately moved to the old self-chiding:

> Do you not come your tardy son to chide,
> That, laps'd in time and passion, lets go by
> Th' important acting of your dread command?
>
> (3.4.106–08)

before he softens to concern for Gertrude, "How is it with you, lady?" (3.4.115). Once the ghost leaves, Hamlet returns, in a way that is painful to Gertrude, to urging her to break off relations with Claudius. To her dazed, "What shall I do?" (3.4.180), Hamlet replies offensively,

> Not this, by no means, that I bid you do.
> Let the bloat king tempt you again to bed,
> Pinch wanton on your cheek, call you his mouse
>
> (3.4.181–83)

By the end of the scene, Hamlet's anger is spent and reduces itself to the indirection of irony as he turns to the body of the dead Polonius, "This counselor/Is now most still, most secret, and most grave" (3.4.213–14).

CHOLERIC LOVESICKNESS

Hamlet's anger is commented on in the play not only by Claudius, who fears that "the hatch and the disclose/ Will be some danger" (3.1.166–67), but by Hamlet himself, in his words to Laertes, in the concluding act of the play,

> For though I am not splenitive [and] rash,
> Yet have I in me something dangerous,
> Which let thy wiseness fear.
>
> (5.1.261–63)

It also has been observed by scholars of Elizabethan literature, beginning with A. C. Bradley, who speaks of "the painful features of his character, . . . his almost savage irritability on the one hand, and on the other his self-absorption, his callousness, his insensibility . . . to the feelings even of those whom he loves" (105–06). Bradley speaks particularly of Hamlet's cruelty to Ophelia, "the disgusting and insulting grossness of his language to her in the play-scene. . . . language as you will find addressed to a woman by no other hero of Shakespeare's" (90).

John Charles Bucknill, the highly respected physician, was a near-contemporary of Bradley's. His *Mad Folk of Shakespeare* predates Bradley's lectures on the tragedies (1904) as well as Ernest Jones's classic essay on Hamlet and Oedipus (1910) and contains observations on the quality of Hamlet's anger that are not only germane to this discussion but anticipate views expressed in the more famous work of Bradley and Wilson.

Bucknill's comments on the other major Hamlet-Ophelia dialogue, the nunnery scene, not only coincide with Bradley's views about Hamlet's harshness to Ophelia in the play scene but touch on a view developed at length in the 1950's by Wilson (101–08): that is, that Hamlet is so harsh because he knows he is talking not only to Ophelia but to Polonius and the others who are hiding. I present Bucknill's observations in full because they have hitherto escaped notice:

> He has before shewn his repugnance to the idea that he is love-sick mad. He knows that Polonius thus explains his conduct; and his harshness to Ophelia is addressed to Polonius, and to any others who may be hiding, more than to Ophelia herself. Yet the harshest words are the true reflex of the morbid side of his mind, which passion and suspicion have cast into the bitterest forms of expression. The true melancholy and the counterfeit madness are strangely commingled in this scene. The latter is shewn by disjointed exclamations and half reasonings. "Ha, ha, are you honest?" "Are you fair?" "I did love you once." "I loved you not" etc., and by the wild form in which the melancholy is here cast. "Get thee to a nunnery: why wouldst thou be a breeder of sinners?" "what

should such fellows as I do crawling between earth and heaven!" "Where's your father?" Ophelia tells a white lie. "At home, my lord." Hamlet knows better and sends a random shaft into his ambuscade. "Let the doors be shut upon him, that he may play the fool nowhere but in this own house." (*The Mad Folk*, 90–91)

Bucknill's comment later in this passage, "the latter part of the speech is directed to the Queen in ambush" [that is, "I say, we will have no more marriages."], returns us to the scene Bradley singles out for Hamlet's high level of cruelty to Ophelia, the play scene. Bucknill is not so troubled by what Bradley considers Hamlet's insulting language to Ophelia:

> The manners and playhouse licence of the time explain the broad indelicacy of the latter; but that he so publicly indulged it may be accepted as proof of his desire to mark his indifference to the woman who had, as he thought, heartlessly jilted him, and whose love he had reason to think had been "as brief as the posy of a ring." (*The Mad Folk*, 94)

Interestingly, Bucknill has nothing to say about the possible effect of the Queen's presence on Hamlet's behavior in the scene, a matter of great significance to Freud and his disciple, Ernest Jones.

They both have made much of this matter—Jones quite directly and fully:

> A case might even be made out for the view that part of his courtship originated not so much in direct attraction for Ophelia as in an unconscious desire to play her off against his mother. . . . When, for instance, in the play scene he replies to his mother's request to sit by her with the words "No, good mother, here's metal more attractive" and proceeds to lie at Ophelia's feet, we seem to have a direct indication of this attitude; and his coarse familiarity and bandying of ambiguous jests with the woman he has recently so ruthlessly jilted are hardly intelligible unless we bear in mind that they were carried

out under the heedful gaze of the Queen. . . . His extraordinary outburst of bawdiness on this occasion, so unex-
pected in a man of obviously fine feeling, points unequi-
vocally to the sexual nature of the underlying turmoil.[7]

If Jones is correct about the sexual nature of Hamlet's
turmoil, that might place in an entirely new light Shakespeare's having Hamlet insist, in the closet scene with
Gertrude, that he is not in the state of ecstacy and that
his pulse "doth temperately keep time" (l. 140), for it
was a commonplace of contemporary Elizabethan psychology that the presence of an intensely desired object
caused the pulse to race. Remember that it was for that
reason that during the Renaissance and, for that matter,
the Middle Ages as well, doctors treating lovesickness
used the increase in pulse rate to determine the identity
of the beloved while various names were spoken in conversation with the patient. Was it Shakespeare's inten-
tion here to depict Hamlet as merely fending off his
mother's suggestion that he is in a manic state, or is
the playwright—cognizant of the psychological commonplace as was his audience—giving us the prince trying to
deflect what would be, within the context of Gertrude's
closet, an appalling suggestion for a possible cause of
mania? If the latter is within the range of plausible interpretation, Shakespeare's psychological insight would certainly count as Freudian before the age of Freud and,
more important, would seem to suggest that Elizabethan
psychology was elastic enough to permit the same sort
of inferences that a psychoanalyst might make with
Freud's system.

Jones's analysis of the play scene is related to a theoretical position on anger and its relationship to melancholia that Freud outlined in his well-known essay,
"Mourning and Melancholia":

> If the object-love, which cannot be given up, takes re-
> fuge in narcissistic identification, while the object it-
> self is abandoned, then hate is expended upon this new

substitute-object, railing at it, depreciating it, making it suffer and deriving sadistic gratification from its suffering. The self-torments of melancholiacs, which are without doubt pleasurable, signify, just like the corresponding phenomenon in the obsessional neurosis, a gratification of sadistic tendencies and hate, both of which relate to an object. . . . (*Collected Papers* 4:161–62)

According to this key passage in Freud's thinking on the subject of melancholia, Hamlet's nihilistic ideas, expressed at various points in the play, would be explained as the result of a shifting of the libido and the sense of loss on to the ego. His theory would also account for the ambivalence of Hamlet's desiring Claudius's death and reproaching himself for not bringing it about. Freud's position on melancholia that, in the most extreme cases, the ego may so punish itself as to cause its own death by suicide was taken up by his disciple. In Jones's view, Hamlet is free to kill Claudius only when he himself is mortally wounded and the Queen is dead, since before that, Hamlet's own repressed desire to possess Gertrude would have made killing Claudius like killing himself (102–03). Jones's idea seems to derive as well from his consideration of a note in Freud's *Interpretation of Dreams*, where Freud speaks of Hamlet's delay in accomplishing the task set by his father's ghost: "The loathing which ought to drive him to revenge is . . . replaced in him by self-reproaches, by conscientious scruples, which represent to him that he himself is no better than the murderer whom he is to punish" (225).

Ella Freeman Sharpe, a lay analyst, adds another interesting twist or two in the application of Freud's description of the mechanism of melancholy to *Hamlet*. Building on the idea in "Mourning and Melancholia" that the psychically incorporated lost beloved person becomes in the mourner an accusing force of conscience, Sharpe argues that Hamlet, who has both recently lost his father and is full of self-accusation, is a clear instance of melancholia. Her particular innovation is to emphasize that

Hamlet should not be confused with the mind of Shakespeare in its confrontation with the death of his father (Sharpe, 203–13). As she says, "The poet is not Hamlet. Hamlet is what he might have been if he had not written the play of *Hamlet*" (cited by Holland, 91). Her consideration of melancholia in Hamlet does not neglect the part that mourning plays in this portrait, as Hamlet's delay is viewed as his attempt to give his mind the time it needs to adjust to loss and a sign of effort waged against the reproaches of his own ego. Juliana Schiesari, in her recent 1992 psychoanalytic study of melancholia, likewise emphasizes the process of recuperating the ego's expenditure of libido in the lost object, which not only takes time but constitutes what Freud considered the necessary "work" of mourning (37).

Yet another supplement to the Freud-Jones oedipal cornerstone is that of the psychoanalyst, Erik Erikson, for whom Hamlet is a delayed adolescent trying to find his true identity. Erikson takes the view that Hamlet's developmental crisis is complicated by what he calls "identity diffusion," which results from the fact that the other five young men in the play are "all sure (or even over-defined) in their identities as dutiful sons, courtiers, and future leaders" but are, nonetheless, like Hamlet, "drawn into the moral swamp of infidelity, which seeps into the fiber of all those who owe allegiance to 'rotten' Denmark."[8] In a world with nothing to be faithful to, Erikson argues, Hamlet becomes a player with "negative identity." In relating Hamlet's melancholy ultimately to a problem of identity, Erikson's view harmonizes with the recent thinking of the literary critic, Stephen Greenblatt, who in his study, *Renaissance Self-Fashioning*, speaks of "the revelation of Hamlet's innermost thought" as "a highly formal *quaestio* on the problem of being and nonbeing" (87).

Shakespeare, in the words he gives Hamlet on the subject of psychological complexes—he uses the Elizabethan term "complexion"—is every bit as ingenious as Freud or

Jones without being so specific about the underlying cause of his particular problem:

> So, oft it chances in particular men,
> That for some vicious mole of nature in them,
> As in their birth, wherein they are not guilty
> (Since nature cannot choose his origin),
> By their o'ergrowth of some complexion,
> Oft breaking down the pales and forts of reason,
> Or by some habit, that too much o'er-leavens
> The form of plausive manners—that these men,
> Carrying, I say, the stamp of one defect,
> Being Nature's livery, or Fortune's star,
> His virtues else, be they as pure as grace,
> As infinite as man may undergo,
> Shall in the general censure take corruption
> From that particular fault.
>
> (1.4.23–36)

In the end Shakespeare proves to be the most eloquent of all the physicians. Hamlet's capacity for introspection is one he shares with other Shakespearian characters, no doubt, because they all share the gift with their creator. It was Coleridge who asserted that "the character of Hamlet may be traced to Shakespeare's deep and accurate science in mental philosophy" (136). One of the most haunting lines in all Shakespeare is Macbeth's question to the doctor, "Canst thou not minister to a mind diseas'd?" (5.3.40), who answers, "Therein the patient/ Must minister to himself" (5.3.45–46).

Six

The Creativity of Influence

An Epilogue

C haucer and Shakespeare were creators capable of original invention and of observing human nature for themselves, but, as members of the medieval and Renaissance worlds respectively, they also derived knowledge about humankind from earlier and contemporary writers, many of whom were themselves indebted to classical thought. Medieval respect for authority was a habit of mind—we see it in Chaucer's highly educated physician pilgrim, who has read all the right books, as well as in the companionable Wife of Bath, who cites her biblical and ecclesiastical authorities, however confusedly, telling stories along the same road to Canterbury. The conclusion of the simplified *Regimen Sanitatis Salernitanum*, known as the *Gouernayle of Helthe*—a late medieval treatise on general hygiene as it appears in the

fifteenth century version of one of the Sloane manuscripts (MS 989)—lists principal authorities of the Middle
Ages, some of whom appear also in the list of Chaucer's
Doctor of Physic and continued to be revered throughout
the Renaissance:

> This lytel booke compiled a worthi clerke called John de
> Burdeux for a frende that he had after the descripcion of
> mani oder diuerse doctours that is to saye, Bernard
> Austyn Plato Tholome Sidrac Arystotell Auycen Galyen
> and Ypocras amany oder diu[er]se acording to the same.
> (*The Gouernayle of Helthe*, 10)

There is a reflection of this compiler's attention to his
revered sources in Chaucer's discriminating attention to
the authorities he used, as Walter Clyde Curry observes:

> Certain passages in Chaucer's work, which may seem to
> be more or less disconnected fragments torn at random
> from some ancient scientific treatise and thrust into the
> smooth flow of a story, often represent in reality the
> most careful selection of pertinent details from a well-
> known body of universally accepted scientific principles.
> (Curry, xi)

Chaucer's writing, as we have seen in the preceding
chapters on his *Book of the Duchess* and *Troilus and Criseyde,* indicates considerable medical knowledge. Anyone who has read Chaucer's dream visions, for instance,
or thought about what Chauntecleer and Pertelote have
to say about dreams, could not fail to see the poet's
fascination with their psychology. That Chaucer read
what he could of dream visions by other poets and about
the scientific side of the question as well in the writings
of "grete clerkys" (*House of Fame* 3.52) is reasonable to
suppose knowing what we do about how writers proceed
when they are interested in a subject. Chaucer scholarship, moreover, in this area is rich in evidence. On the
depth of the poet's curiosity about dreams, no one is
more convincing than the voice of the poet himself:

> God turne us every drem to goode!
> For hyt is wonder, be the roode,
> To my wyt, what causeth swevenes
> Eyther on morwes or on evenes;
> And why th' effect folweth of somme,
> And of somme hit shal never come;
> Why that is an avisioun
> And this a revelacion,
> Why this a drem, why that a sweven, . . .
>
> *(House of Fame* 1.1–9)

For 51 lines the poet entertains a variety of ideas about what might have caused his dream: the complexions may have caused it, or it may have proceeded from a feebleness or disturbance of the brain, or from too much study or prayer or contemplation, or from a prophetic power in the soul.

In short, Chaucer was a thinker as well as a poet. He thought, asked questions and sought answers, be the intellectual problem at hand dreams or melancholy or other familiar areas of Chaucerian speculation: fate, predestination, nature and so on. Apart from the hundreds of medical works in Merton College, Oxford, St. Augustine's Abbey at Canterbury, Christ Church, Canterbury and Dover Priory, extant in Chaucer's day (Robbins, "The Physician's Authorities," 341), there were learned contemporary physicians whom he probably knew. Huling Ussery reminds us that "he served in the households of great nobles and was acquainted with their physicians and surgeons; he himself was of a class that would ordinarily be expected to use their services" (18). As Chaucer was interested in medical matters, had access to great libraries, and was acquainted with the physicians of royal households, it satisfies our expectations to find his poetry contains evidence of profound thought and learning about melancholy, a subject as fundamental as it is inescapable in human life. His poems concerning melancholy reveal an eloquent voice that speaks for his age, looks forward to humoural psychology on stage, and remains a voice that can still be heard and understood in our day.

The preceding chapters devoted to Shakespeare's treatment of melancholy demonstrate that his knowledge of physiology and psychology was as profound as Chaucer's. Like Chaucer, Shakespeare was acquainted with contemporary science and scientists (including his own son-in-law, John Hall, who practiced medicine in Stratford). He looked at nature with a penetrating and comprehensive vision wherein poetry and science met in ways that reveal the thought of his age and attest to his remarkable understanding of medical material. Most medical references in the plays are brief, like Falstaff's exposition of the physiological effects of sherry in *Henry IV, Part 2*, but often passages are protracted. The subject of Helena's cure of the French king's fistula, for instance, remains a focus of *All's Well that Ends Well* for the first two acts of the play, and Mistress Quickly's description of Falstaff's death in *Henry V* contains clinical details both poignant and accurate on the movement of the old knight's hands, the sharp look of his nose, his delirious talk, and finally, the coldness of his extremities in the last hour of his life:

'A parted ev'n just between twelve and one, ev'n
at the turning o' th' tide; for after I saw him
fumble with the sheets, and play with flowers,
and smile upon his finger's end, I knew there
was but one way; for his nose was as sharp as
a pen, and 'a [babbl'd] of green fields. . . . So
'a cried out, "God, God, God!" three or four times.
Now I, to comfort him, bid him 'a should not
think of God; I hop'd there was no need to
trouble himself with any such thoughts yet.
So 'a bade me lay more clothes on his feet.
I put my hand into the bed and felt them,
and they were as cold as any stone.

(2.3.12–24)

The passage may bespeak firsthand acquaintance with deathbed experience, but most of the details turn up in fifteenth and sixteenth century popular medical books containing descriptions of the signs of death. Such books were common possessions in middle class households in Shakespeare's day, and he was doubtless familiar with some of them. More importantly, he was able to do much with little.

The literary treatments of melancholy from Chaucer and Shakespeare examined in this study present the condition in terms of its human aspects, not just psychological and physiological, but also moral and philosophical. Even the best of the classical, medieval and Renaissance medical treatises are limited to prose descriptions of causes, symptoms and remedies, repeated from medical author to medical author as they are handed down through the ages. In Chaucer's narrative poems, *The Book of the Duchess* and *Troilus and Criseyde,* and in Shakespeare's poetic dramas, *As You Like It* and *Hamlet,* we see causes, symptoms and remedies take on the complexity of life as poets breathe spirit into science; overlapping views of the human—the bereaved, the lovesick, the unhappy thinker—are inspired with art. In the pragmatic prose of the medical treatises we find the diseases—melancholy, mania, *amor hereos*—flowing one into the other with the tedium of lists which seem to repeat from disease to disease. The early poets and physicians agree about what melancholy is, but only the poets help us see its human face and give expression to melancholy as a condition of mortality. In concluding this study, it can be said that while melancholy asserts itself in times of crisis as a response to loss or bereavement, poets seem to be nourished by the sorrow it causes in others or themselves, and are able to give it words.

NOTES

Notes to Chapter 1

1. See passage cited on p. 80. In his biography of Bernard, Demaitre comments on the doctor's literary background, evidenced by "extensive quotations from poetry as well as from the Bible" (14), noting that in his works he names among classical authors "Pythagoras, Sallust, Horace, Ovid, Seneca, and Boethius" (16), the backbone of the medieval curriculum in the trivium.

2. Other recent notable studies of melancholy are Tellenbach's *Melancholy: History of the Problem* . . . and Pigeaud's *La Maladie de L'Âme.*

3. Her source is the Carthusian *Tractatus de regimine sanitatis virorum spiritualium ac devotorum* (12–21) edited by Manfred P. Koch (18) in his dissertation *Das "Erfurter Kartauserregimen."*

4. She cites from Henry Cuffe's *The Differences of the Ages of Man's Life.* In his recent book, *The Ages of Man*, J. A. Burrow emphasizes the spiritual benefits of old age—"Although wisdom and virtue may never be out of season, it is only in old age that they can be deemed positively natural" (151).

5. A recent article by Hans Biesterfeldt and Dimitri Gutas demonstrates that the most authoritative form of the *Problem* (for the *Problemata Physica*), the Aristotelian, is related to an Alexandrian version that may have been compiled in Olympiodorus between the fourth and seventh centuries (22).

6. J. C. Ackerman, introduction to the Galen volume in *Medicorum Graecorum Opera Quae Exstant*, (*Opera* Claudii Galeni), ed. D. Carolus Gottlob Kühn. (Lipsiae: Libraria Car. Cnoblochii, 1821), xcviii–c.

7. The Latin text can be found in *Pauli Aeginetae Libri Tertii Interpretatio Latina Antiqua*, cap. LXII, "De Melancolia et Mania et Enteasticis," 33: "Melancolia desipientia quedam est sine febre ex melancolico maxime humore facta occupante intellectum, aliquando quidem ipso prius patiente cerebro, aliquando uero toto intercepto corpore."

8. *Pauli Aeginetae Libri Tertii . . .*, capitulum LVIII, "Cvratio Melancholie," 34. The relevant Latin is "Eos igitur qui secundum principalem passionem cerebri melancholici sunt et per laucra assidua et dietam boni humoris et humidam curare, simul secundum animam conpetenti exilaratione."

9. *Pauli Aeginetae Libri Tertii . . .*, 35: "post flebotamiam uero refectum inferius purgare ex siconia et nigro elleboro, et emorroidas asperiamus et menstrua prouocemus, si propter horum retentionem sit facta passio."

10. The English translations in the body of my text are mine unless otherwise indicated. Oribasius, *Synopseos ad Evastathium Filium Libri Novem*, liber VIII, cap. X:

> Quos hoc malum in*f*estos habet: nocturno tempore domo egressi lupos in rebus omnibus imitantur: & ad diem usque circa tumulos vagantur mortuorum. hos ita cognosces pallidi sunt, oculos hebetes & siccos, non illacrymantes, eos*que* concavos habent. lingua sicissima est, nulla penitus in ore saliva conspicitur, siti evecti sunt, crura vero, quia noctu saepe offendunt, sine remedio exulcerata. hae sunt illorum notae. qua in re sciendum est, lycanthropiam esse melancholiae speciem: quam accessionis tempore curabis secta vena, & facta usque ad animi defectionem vacuatione:. . . . deinde sero lactis per triduum usus, etiam hiera ex colocynthide semel, bis, & ter purgabis. Post purgationes theriacen ex viperis dato. & item alia quae in melancholiae curatione sunt commemorata. Morbo invadente aeger perspergendus est iis, quae somnum conciliare consueverunt. ubi vero somnus accesserit, aures & nares opio illinantur.

An interesting general study on the subject is the picturesque compendium of post-fifteenth century medical cases, trial records and legends, *A Lycanthropy Reader: Werewolves in Western Culture*, ed. Charlotte Otten.

11. Haly Abbas, *Liber Totius Medicine*, "Theorice," cap. VII:

> Melancholia nigra animi est profusio sine febre: quae aut propter cerebri fit passiones ipsius aut eius cum membris

aliis quamvis in passione pro participanti. Et quae ex ipsius cerebri fit passione ex nigri colici humoris coadunatione est quae in ipso nascitur aut ad ipsum ab huius passionis stomacho ascendit: coadunantur quoque in eo paulatim: sitque eiusmodi res manifesta: cum qui insunt aduruntur humores: unde anima turbatur & cogitatio diminuitur. Quae autem pro participationis fit causu cerebri cum aliis membris: quidam ex vaporibus nigris fit humoribus qui a stomacho ad cerebrum ascendunt ab humoribus qui in ipso exuruntur et locis quibus hypochondriis subsunt dicitur passio haec ascendens. Quaedam ab his fit qui ex omni corpore ad ipsum ascendunt adustis humoribus. Nonumquam autem passio haec ex timore oritur et tristitia. Et communia omibusque desipientia patiuntur nigra signa sunt tristitia, timor, opinio mala. Et quidem quibus accidit mortem timent: quidam desiderant: quidam risum multiplicant: nonnulli fletum: et alii seipsos abnegant et se non esse dicunt quidam vasse esse fictile arbitrantur: ideoque ne frangantur precavent. Alii irrationlium aliquod [ee] se animalium putant: et animalis illius voce clamant. Alii vates se predicant & futura se predicere dicunt.

Constantine the African translated the work of Ali ibn al-Abbas as the *Pantegni*, which comprise the *pars theorica* (10 books) and the *pars practica* (also 10 books). The *Liber totius medicine* is the title given to a second translation of the work in 1127 by Stephen of Antioch. Thus the text cited here from "Haly Abbas" is probably not Constantine's version, but Stephen's.

12. The *De Melancholia* has been published in a facing-page Latin/Arabic parallel text edition by Karl Garbers as *Libri Duo De Melancholia*. The Latin text is Constantine's translation from the 1536 Basel edition and the Arabic text is that of Ishaq ibn Imran.

13. Constantinus Africanus, *Opera* (Basle, 1536), 1:288: "Alii . . . amant solitudinem et obscuritatem et ab hominibus remotionem. Alii spatiosa loca amant et lucida atque pratosa, hortos fructiferos, aquosos. Alii amant equitare, diversa musicorum genere audire, loqui quoque cum sapientibus vel amabilibus . . . Alii habent nimium somnum, alii plorant, alii rident."

14. Africanus, *Opera*, 283–84:

Sufficit nobis dixisse de causa corporis, uel melancholiae.

> Oportet ergo utpote promisimus, eam quae est secundum animam dicamus. Habet igitur anima actiones suas mutabiles, sicut de ira, in pacationem:. . . . Huiiusmodi melancholiae sunt vicini, propter inuestigationem scientiae, & fatigationem suae memoriae, & tristitiam de animae suae defectione, & propter intentionis suae complementum ac firmamentum. Omnia haec memoriam eorum deficere faciunt & rationem, ac intellectum. Sicut dixit Hippocrates in epidemiarum libreis sexta particula: Animae, inquit, labor est cogitatio. [Sicut est corporis labor ambulare, quare pessimos generat morbos, utpote corporis labor.]

15. Dante Alighieri, *Inferno* in *The Divine Comedy* (Italian text and translation), trans. and ed. Charles Singleton, 1.45: "Euclid the geometer, and Ptolemy, Hippocrates, Avicenna, Galen, and Averroes, who made the great commentary."

16. Geoffrey Chaucer, *The Riverside Chaucer*, 3rd ed., *General Prologue* of *The Canterbury Tales*, lines 429–34. All quotations from Chaucer's poetry are drawn from this text.

17. Avicenna, trans. Gerardo Carmonensi postea uero aba Andrea Alpago, *Liber Canonis*, I, I, 4, cap. 1, 14:

> Melancholia uero non naturalis, . . . est ad modum adustionis & cineereitatis. . . . Melancholia aute quae est superflues, alia est quae est cinis cholerae, & adustionis eius: & ipsa est amara inter quam tamen & choleram rubeam qum adustam uo camus, existit differentia, quod illa est cholera rubea, cui cinis hic fuit admistus: haec uero non est nisi cinis per se separatus, cuius subtile fuit resolutum. Alia est quae cinis phlegmatis, & quod de eo adustum fuit: & si phlegma ualde subtile & aquosum fuerit, eius cinis erit salsus: & sinon, trahit ad acredinem aut poticitatem. Alia est quae est cinis sanguinis, & haec quidum est salsa, ad paucum trahens dulcedinem. Alia est quae est cinis melancholiae naturalis: quae si subtilis fuerit, erit eius cinis, & quod de ea adustum est, ualde acre, sicut acetum, quod cum super terrae faciem cadit, ebullit: & eius odor est acris, a quo muscae fugiunt, & alia: & si grossa fuerit, minoris erit acredimis cum ponticitate & amaritudine. Malae igitur cholerae nigra species sunt tres: cholera rubea cum aduritur, & eius subtile resoluitur: & duae aliae diuisiones, quas post eam diximus. Melancholia uero phlegmatica est tardioris nocumenti, & minoris malitiae. Et melancholia cholerica est, que est

fortioris malitiae, & uelocioris corruptionis. Vernunta-
men est susceptibilior curationis, quam illae.

18. Avicenna, *Liber Canonis*, III, I, 4, cap. 19, 377:

Et dicimus quod cholera nigra faciens melancholiam,
cum est cum sanguine, est cum gaudio et risu et non
concomitatur ipsam tristitia vehemens. Si autem est cum
phlegmate est cum pigritia et paucitate motus et quiete.
Et si est cum cholera vel ex cholera est cum agitatione et
aliquali daemonio et est similis maniae. Et si fuerit cholera nigra pura, tunc cogitatio in ipsa erit plurima et
agitatio seu furiositas erit minus: nisi moveatur et rixetur
et habeat odium cuius non obliviscitur.

19. *The Wyse Boke of Maystyr Peers of Salerne*, folio 3r; the
manuscript is a fifteenth century copy. My edition of this
work is forthcoming from *Manuscripta*.
20. *Renart le Contrefait*, II: "I cited Galen and expounded
old works of Razis and Avicenna." Cited and translated by
Mann, *Medieval Estates Satire*, 92–93.
21. *Renart le Contrefait*, II: "and together with the doctor, I
played the astronomer. I named signs and points and the
positions of the constellations, the planets, and the figures;"
Mann, 93–94.
22. *Hamlet, The Riverside Shakespeare*. My attention was
drawn to this and one or two of the other Shakespearean passages by Kellogg, 5–8. Throughout this book, quotations from
Shakespeare refer to *The Riverside Shakespeare*.

Notes to Chapter 2

1. John Livingston Lowes, 491–546. The use of *amor
hereos* has been explored by D. W. Robertson, Jr., *A Preface to
Chaucer*, 457–63; by Ciavolella in *La "Malattia D'Amore"
dall'Antichità al Medioevo*; by Wack in two articles, "New
Medieval Medical Texts on *Amor Hereos*," 288–98 and "The
Liber de heros morbo of Johannes Afflacius . . . ," 324–44; and
in *Lovesickness in the Middle Ages: The Viaticum and Its
Commentaries*; and by Jacquart and Thomasset. A brief but
germane note of my own is "That Dog Again: *Melancholia
Canina* and Chaucer's *Book of the Duchess*," 185–90.
2. Caelius Aurelianus is quoted in several medieval glos-
saries and (without citation) in Isidore of Seville's *Origines*; he
appears in two ninth century library catalogs of the monastery

of Lorsch (Drabkin, Introduction, 12), in a tenth century catalog from Verona (Beccaria, *I Codici Di Medicina Del Periodo Presalernitano*, 56).

3. The Latin is "saxo tamen exit ab imo/rivus aquae Lethes, per quem cum murmure labens/invitat somnos crepitantibus unda lapillis./ante fores antri fecunda papavera florent/ innumeraeque herbae, quarum de lacte soporem/Nox legit et spargit per opacas umida terras" (162).

4. The most celebrated of the numerous Latin translations is that of Cornarius, published in *Medicae Artis Principes* by Henry Stephens. Later, in the sixteenth century, the sixth book of his *Epitome Medica* was published in French at Lyons (1539), and the original Greek appears in two editions, one the Aldine (1529) and one the Basle (1538) [See Adams's introduction to Aegineta's *Seven Books*, 3, 16.]

5. The Latin text is in *Pauli Aeginetae Libri Tertii*, cap. LVII, "De Melancolia et Mania et Enteasticis," 33: "Propria uero signa [sunt] . . . insomnietates."

6. *Pauli Aeginetae Libri Tertii*, cap. LXII, "De Cupidinibus," 38: "hos igitur [sunt] tristes et uigilantes."

7. *Pauli Aeginetae Libri Tertii*, cap. LXII, 38: "Cerebri passionibus cupidines adiungere nichil inconueniens, cum sint sollicitudines quedam. Sollicitudo uero passio est anime in motu laborioso constituta ratione."

8. Rhazes, *Continens . . . ordinatus & Correctus per . . . Hieronymous Surinanus*. Liber Primus, Tractatus XX, cap. I, fol. XXIIIr:

> Dixit Judaeus quod pacientes coturub vel ereos incedunt de nocte tamquam canes: et eorum facies sunt crocee propter vigilias. . . .
>
> Dixit Alexander quod pacientes coturub vel ereos incedent stridendo atque vagando et clamando tota nocte et praecipue per sepulturas mortuorum usque ad mane.

9. Rhazes, *Liber divisionum* in *Opera Parva* (Venice, 1537), "De cucubut," cap. X, fol. VIv: "Est species una que fit ex adustione sanguinis: et signa eius sunt vehementia submissionis faciei: et tristitia assidua et taciturnitas et alleviatio in nocte." The tracts of Rhazes in this volume also appeared in the Venice 1500 edition of the *Liber Almansoris*, Klebs, no. 8263, where it is described as a reprint of the 1497 edition. That of Milan, 1481, contained several of these tracts.

10. Rhazes, cap. X, fol. VIv, "Et cura eius est cura melancolie

qui est ex dominio melancolie in toto corpore: et multitudo administrationis olei et balneum et medicine somnum facientes ex eis quae effunduntur supra caput: sicut decoctio seminis lactuce: et cortice papaueris et violarum siccatarum et emulgere lac supra caput: et cibi facti ex lactura et cucurbita cum oleo amigdalino."

11. Bernard of Gordon, *Omnium Aegritudinem a Vertice ad Calcem. Opus Praeclarissimus quod Lilium Medicinae* (1542), "De mania & melancholia," cap. 19, fol. 106v–110v; "De amore qui hereos dicitur," cap. 20, fol. 111r–112v.

12. Bernard, "De amore . . .," fol. 111r: "Signa autem sunt quando amittunt somnum, cibum, potum, & maceratur totum corpus, praeterquam oculi, & habent cogitationes occultas profundas, cum suspiriis luctuosis."

13. Bernard, "De Mania . . .," fol. 109r: ". . . competunt in curatione omnia humectantia, cum passio sit propter siccum, & ideo competit sibi somnus, quies, ocium. . . ."

14. Valescus de Taranta, *Philonium aurem ac perutile opus practice medicine opera dantibus: quod Philonium appellatur,* Liber Primus, cap. xi, "De Amore hereos," fol. 11r; cap. xii, "De Mania," fol. 11v.

15. A good discussion of the "lawe of kinde" may be found in Robert Burlin, 64–66, and in Lynn V. Sadler, 51–64.

16. Roger S. Loomis, "Chaucer's Eight Years' Sickness," 178–80, and Robinson, "Explanatory Notes," 773. See also James Wimsatt, *Chaucer and the French Love Poets,* 116, on the pattern of portraying a wife as a courtly mistress as in Machaut's *Fonteinne Amoureuse.*

17. Olson translates the Latin, "*Confabulator* debut autem recitator fabularum boni esse intellectus in scientiis ipsius generis fabularum in quibus delectatur animus. . . ." from "Traites d'hygiene du moyen age," ed. Leopold Delisle, 534.

18. Bruno Bettelheim, for instance, writes in *The Uses of Enchantment,* that for a story to enrich a child's life, "it must stimulate his imagination; help him to develop his intellect and to clarify his emotions; be attuned to his anxieties and aspirations; give full recognition to his difficulties, while at the same time suggesting solutions to the problems which perturb him" (5). He could almost be describing the cathartic experience the narrator-dreamer, Alcyone, and the black knight undergo in the course of *The Book of the Duchess.*

19. In *Pauli Aeginetae Libri Tertii,* the relevant passage is in cap. LXII, "De Cupidinibus," 38: "hos igitur tristes et vigilantes ignorantes quidam dispositionem abstinentia

balneorum et silentius et tenui dieta affecerunt; in quibus considerantes sapientiores amantem et ad lauacra et ad uini potionem et ad deambulationes et spectacula et auditiones mentem de-duxerunt."

20. Avicenna, *Liber Canonis...* (1486), lib. III, Fen. I, Tractatus IV, cap. xxv, "De Cura." This work was originally translated from the Arabic into Latin by Gerard of Cremona (1114–1187). Avicenna's ideas on melancholia derive from Haly Abbas.

21. Anglicus, *On the Properties of Things: John of Trevisa's translation* . . . I, Lib. Septimus, cap. 7, 350; Liber Quintus, cap. 23, 212. This encyclopedia was popular and translated into several languages between the middle of the thirteenth century until the seventeenth century.

22. Avicenna, *Liber Canonis*, Lib. III, Fen. I, Tractatus IV, cap. xxv.

23. *On the Properties of Things.* I; Lib. Septimus, cap. 7, 350; Lib. Quintus, cap. 23, 212.

24. This view is well represented by Wolfgang Clemen in *Chaucer's Early Poetry*, 42–49.

25. In *"Mutatio Amoris"*: *"Penitentia" and the Form of The Book of the Duchess,"* R. A. Shoaf uses literary and theological sources to define the role of penitential imagery in the poem. He observes that the Dreamer describes the Black Knight's problem as "shryfte wythoute repentaunce," but that the Black Knight cannot repent past love for that would seem to betray it. The penitential perspective sheds more light on the content of the talk than on its form.

26. Bernard, fol. 11v: "Patiens iste aut est obediens rationi, aut non. Si est obediens, remoueatur ab illa falsa ymaginatione, ab aliquo viro quem timeat, de quo verecundetur cum verbis & admonitionibus, ostendendo pericula seculi, diem iudicii, & gaudia paradisi."

27. Bernard, fol. 11v: "tamen dicit Avicenna quod aliqui sunt, qui gaudent in audiendo foetida & illicita. Queratur igitur vetula turpissima in aspectu cum magnis dentibus & barba, & cum turpi & vili habitu."

28. Johannes Anglicus de Gaddesden, *Rosa Anglica Practica Medicine* (1492), fol. 132v: "Sed in amore ereos oportet vituperare illam quam diligit."

29. Bernard, fol. 108v: "Primum enim quod competit in curatione omnium maniacorum, est gaudium & laetitia, quoniam illud quod magis nocet est solicitudo, & tristitia, & ideo domus debet esse clara, luminosa, sine picturis & debent ibi esse multa odorifera. . . ."

30. Bernard, fol. 108v: "... omnes habitantes in ea debent esse pulchri aspectus, & omnes quos timeat & de quibus verecundetur si enormia egerit, aut fatua loquaeretur, & ipsi debent multa promittere."

31. Bernard, fol. 111v: "Vtile igitur est mutare regimen, & esse inter amicos & notos, & quod vadat per loca vbi sint prata, fontes, montes, nemora, odores boni, pulcrhi aspectus, cantus avium, instrumenta musica."

32. Rhazes, "De Coturub vel ereos," in *Continens*, liber primus tractatus 20, fol. xciii[r] in *Opera Parva* ... (1537). *Coturub* is the same as *cutubut*, the Arabic word for *melancholia canina* and Ereos [*hereos*].

33. *Calendar of the Patent Rolls Preserved in the Public Record Office...*, Richard II, A.D. *1385–1389*, 324. The fourteenth century treatise of medical prose, *The Wyse Boke of Maystyr Peers of Salerne.* may be his, and was very likely known to Chaucer, judging from echoes in his own *Treatise on the Astrolabe* (see p. 27).

Notes to Chapter 3

1. The most eloquent detractor is E. Talbot Donaldson, "The Myth of Courtly Love," *Speaking of Chaucer*, 154–63.

2. Important in understanding some of the controversial issues are: Denomy, C. S. B., *The Heresy of Courtly Love*; Benton, "Clio and Venus: An Historical View of Medieval Love"; Boase, *The Origin and Meaning of Courtly Love*; Menocal, *The Arabic Role in Medieval Literary History: A Forgotten Heritage*. David Aers is, as far as I know, the first to explain the phenomenon in economic terms (in *Chaucer, Langland, and the Creative Imagination*, 119): "The formula of an outstanding knight committing his existence to the devoted service of a woman fulfilled a psychological and perhaps growing need to create a more satisfying alternative to the real organisation of Eros and marriage in medieval society. Customary practices and ideology ... demanded the subordination of women to men and land."

3. The *locus classicus* is Lowes's, "The Loveres Maladye of Hereos"; and Massimo Ciavolella's book, *La Malattia D'Amore Dall'Antichità al Medioevo*, deserves to be better known than it is. Mary Wack's *Lovesickness in the Middle Ages: The Viaticum and Its Commentaries* (1990) is an interesting new study, and Jacquart and Thomasset discuss the disease as "the hysterical malady" and as "suffocation of the womb" in *Sexuality and Medicine in the Middle Ages*,

174–79. See also Wack's "Lovesickness in *Troilus*," 55–61, and my own early version of this chapter which appeared in *Neophilologus* 74 (1990), 294–309.

4. "Signa autem sunt quando amittunt somnum, cibum, potum," (Gordonius); "Et maceratur totum corpus," (Gordonius); "Et oculi concavantur," (Arnaldus); "Et eorum facies sunt croceae propter vigilias," (Rhazes); "Pacientes. . . . ereos incedunt stridendo. . . . et clamando tota nocte," (Rhazes); "Alteratur dispositio ejus. . . . ad tristitiam et fletum, cum amoris cantilenas audit," (Avicenna). For more complete references, see Lowes, 525–26.

5. Bernard, *Lilium Medicinae* (1542), fol. 111v: "Nisi hereosis succuratur, in maniam cadunt vel moriuntur."

6. Arnaldus de Villanova, *Breviarum*, lib. primus, cap. xxvi ("De mania et melancholia"), in *Opera* (1509), fol. 161r: "Mania quidem est infectio anterioris cellulae capitis cum priuatione imaginationis. . . . melancholia: est tristitiae timor: et destructio sermonis: et locus eius. . . . est media cellula capitis inter rationalem et fantasticam."

7. Constantinus Africanus, *Liber de Oblivione* in Isaac Judaeus, *Omnia Opera* (1515), fol. ccixv[erso]:

> operatio mentis triplex est: prima phantasia, secunda rationalis intellectus, tertia memoria. Et cerebri due partes sunt. Una prora: altera puppis. Et prora dividitur in duas partes. . . . Et duo ventriculi prore mutant aerem: ex quo qualiter et dant inde cerebro spiritum animalem ut faciat sensus videndi: audiendi, odorandi, gustandi et iterum phantasiam: deinde transit ad eum locum qui est in medio cerebri qui corporis est: et transit spiritus animalis iam subtilis et mundificatus et clarus plus quam spiritus qui fuit in prora cerebri: ut faciat rationem et intellectum et habeat in capite medii ventriculi qui est inter proram et puppim.

8. Translated by S. Delany, *Chaucer Review* 4 (1970): 55–65.

9. See my article, "Contraception and the Pear Tree Episode of Chaucer's *Merchant's Tale*," *Journal of English and Germanic Philology* 94 (1995): 31–41.

10. John of Trevisa, *On the Properties of Things*, liber quartus, capitulum x, 159; liber quartus, capitulum xi, 161. Such citations suggest that Chaucer could also have gotten knowledge of Constantine indirectly.

11. Arnaldus de Villanova, *De parte operativa*, in *Opera*, fol. 249v: "Hic autem amor furiosus, cum particulare rei

exemplo lucidius pateat inter virum et mulierem, videtur imperio subiugato rationis incendi, propter singularem coytus delectationem."

12. Arnaldus, fol. 249v:

> Cum itaque firma retentio formarum in multis quibus-
> libet nequaquam effici valeat sine sicco, necessario se-
> quitur cerebellarem partem imaginativae virtutis ali-
> qualiter exsiccari. Hoc vero ex praetactis sic ostenditur:
> videtur tamen etiam fortis et frequens sit transitus calo-
> ris spirituum ad cellam aestimativae, fluentium ad iudi-
> cium celebrandum, pars anterior, in qua imaginativa
> residet, propter humoris consumptionem a calore spiritu-
> um relicta, remanet necessario siccius seu minus humida
> quam fuerit.

13. An informative discussion of the development of medical thought on the lover's malady from Constantine's chapter on the disease through Arnaldus's tract appears in Michael R. McVaugh's introduction to his edition of Arnaldus de Villanova's "Tractatus De Amore Heroico" in *Opera Medica Omnia*, 3.14–30.

14. John Benton's "Clio and Venus: An Historical View of Medieval Love" offers an interesting and well-known reexamination of the term.

15. Quoted by James Wilhelm, *The Cruelest Month*, 151, 153.

16. Wilhelm, 188. Subsequent references to the poem may be found here.

17. Michael MacDonald discusses "nakedness" as a frequently cited symptom of mania in ancient and medieval times in his *Mystical Bedlam*, 129–34.

18. Dante Alighieri, *The Divine Comedy* with translation and commentary by Charles S. Singleton, *Inferno* 5.100–08:

> Amor, ch'al cor gentil ratto s'apprende,
> prese costui de la bella persona
> che mi fu tolta; e 'l modo ancor m'offende.
>
> Amor, ch'a nullo amato amar perdona,
> mi prese del costui piacer si forte,
> che, come vedi, ancor non m'abbandona.
>
> Amor condusse noi ad una morte. . . .

19. Arnaldus de Villanova, *De parte operativa*, in *Opera*, fol. 146v: "dispositiones corporis inclinantes ad talem

concupiscentiam propter aliquam utilitatem sine necessitatem, sicut est inter virum et mulierem complexio venerea vel humiditas titillans in organis generationis."

20. Cf. Alexander J. Denomy, *"Fin' Amors:* The Pure Love of the Troubadours, its Amorality, and Possible Source," 189–206, and A. R. Nykl, *The Dove's Neck-Ring,* xc–cl; *Hispano-Arabic Poetry and Its Relations with the Old Provencal Troubadours,* 382–93.

21. Translated in 1974 by Stern as *Hispano-Arabic Strophic Poetry: Studies,* ed. L. P. Harvey.

22. Fackenheim, translator of "A Treatise on Love by Ibn Sina," ch. 5, *On the Love of Those who are Noble-Minded and Young for External Beauty,* 218–22. See also Roger Boase, 65. The chief objection to Avicenna's influence is that there is no evidence that his works were translated into Latin until the 1180s. See Denomy, "Concerning the Accessibility of Arabic influence to the earliest troubadours," 147–58.

23. Avicenna, *Liber Canonis De Medicinis.* . . . translated by Andreas Alpagus (Venetiis [Venice], 1562), fol. 206v:

> Cognitio enim eius quod diligitur est vna viarum curae ipsius, & ingenium in hoc est, vt nomina plura nominentur, iterando multoties, & sit manus super pulsum ipsius. Cumque propter illud diuersificatur diuersitate magna, & sit similis interfecto deinde iterature & experitur illud multoties, scitur quod illud est nomen eius, quod diligitur: . . . Amplius cum non inuenitur cura nisi regimen coniunctionis inter eos secundum modum permissionis fidei et legis, fiat.

24. Bernard, *Lilium Medicinae,* fol. 110v: "[Cur haec passio, hereos a quibusdam nominetur] Hereos dicitur quia hereosi & nobilies propter affluentiam delitiarum, istam passionem consueuerunt incurrere, quoniam sicut dicit Viaticus: Sicut felicitas est ultimum dilectionis, ita hereos vltimum dilectionis & ideo intantum concupiscunt quod insani efficiuntur. Iuxta illud Ouidii: A trabe sublimi, triste pependit onus."

25. Felix Platter, "Praxeos," chapter 3, *Animi Commotio, Observationum Libri Tres* (1641).

26. Bernard, fol. 111v: "deinde tollatur ocium de quo Ouidius: 'Ocia si tollas, periere cupidinis artes.'"

27. *Pauli Aeginetae Libri Tertii,* cap. LXII, "De Cvpidinibvs," 38: "sollicitudo uero passio est anime in motu laborioso constituta ratione. . . . nam studentes semper amori difficile mobilem habent passionem."

28. Bernard, fol. 110v: "Amor qui hereos dicitur est sollicitudo melancolica propter mulieris amorem."

29. Bernard, fol. 110v:

> Causa huius passionis, est corruptio extimatiue, propter formam & figuram fortitier affixam, vnde cum aliquis philocaptus est in amore alicuius mulieris, ita fortiter concipit formam & figuram & modum, quoniam credit & opinatur hanc esse meliorem, pulchriorem & magis vene-rabilem, magis speciosam, & melius dotatam in natura-libus & moralibus, quam aliquam aliarum, & ideo arden-ter concupiscit eam, & sine modo & mensura, opinans si posset finem attingere, quod haec esset sua felicitas, beati-tudo, & intantum corruptum est iudicium rationis, quod continue cogitat de ea, & dimittit omnes suas opera-tiones, ita quod si aliquis loquatur cum eo, vix intelligit aliqua alia Et quia est in continua meditatione, ideo sollicitudo melancolica appellatur.

30. Quoted by Lowes, 506: "et ita continue nocte dieque stant amantium animae ita quod nil aliud perfecte imaginari possunt et deus scit quomodo ratio tunc operatur."

31. Bernard, fol. 111r: "amittunt somnum, cibum, potum"

32. *Pauli Aeginetae Libri Tertii*, cap. LXII, "De Cvpi-dinibvs," 38: "hos igitur [sunt] tristes et uigilantes."

33. Bernard, fol. 112r: "Coitus igitur, quia laetificat & calefacit, & bonam digestionem inducit, ideo bene competit quibus est permissum."

34. *Rosa Anglica*, "De mania desipientia et melancolia," (Venice: Bonetum Locatellum, 1492), fol. 132r: "Ite coitus moderatus ab aliquibus comendatur ad expulsionem maniae a cerebro."

35. Donaldson, "The Ending of Chaucer's *Troilus*," in *Speaking of Chaucer*, 84–101; and Salter, "*Troilus and Criseyde*: a Reconsideration," 86–106.

36. Dante Alighieri, *Paradiso*: "Col viso ritornai per tutte quante/le sette spere, e vidi questo globo/tal, ch'io sorrisi del suo vil sembiante."

37. George Sarton takes Chaucer's linking of Bernard of Gordon, John of Gaddesden and Gilbert the Englishman in the Physician's portrait (*General Prologue*, 434) as evidence of "the accuracy of Chaucer's learning," "Lilium Medicinae," *Mediaeval Studies in Honor of J. D. M. Ford*, eds. Holmes and Denomy, 242. See also Rossell Hope Robbins, 341.

Notes to Chapter 4

1. *The Harvard Concordance to Shakespeare* lists 76 entries for "melancholy," 1 for "melancholies," and 1 for "melancholy's" (809).

2. A translation of the 1610 French version of *Erotomania* has been published (1990) as *A Treatise on Lovesickness/ Jacques Ferrand*, tr. and ed. Massimo Ciavolella and Donald Beecher. This work focuses exclusively on love melancholy. A microfilm copy of the seventeenth century English edition is on file at Harvard's Houghton Library as *Erotomania or A Treatise Discoursing of the Essence, Causes, Symptoms, Prognostics and cure of Love*, written by James [sic] Ferrand (Oxford, England: L. Lichfield, 1640).

3. William Richardson, *A Philosophical Analysis and Illustration of Some of Shakespeare's Remarkable Characters*, 144–76; Bucknill, *The Mad Folk of Shakespeare*, 292–313; A. O. Kellogg, *Shakespeare's Delineations of Insanity, Imbecility and Suicide*, 87–102. The medical textbook Bucknill coauthored with Daniel H. Tuke is *A Manual of Psychological Medicine*.

4. His introduction to *As You Like It* in *The Complete Works of Shakespeare*, 588.

5. Cited by Schleiner (177) and translated from the Latin: Iulius Caesar Scaliger, *Exotericarum exercitationum*, lib. xv, *De subtilitate* (Frankfort, 1576), exercitatio 122 (p. 422):

> Cervi lachrymam, rem fortasse minus tibi notam, in nostris Musarum thesauris habemus charissimam. Ante centesimum annum in cervo nulla est. Post eam aetatem accrescit ad oculi canthum, ipsis ossibus, atque in os protuberans concrescit, ea duritia, qua cornu superet. Qua parte prominet, rotunda est, insigni nitore coloris fulvi, non sine vestigiis atriorum venularum. Tanta laevitate, ut pene tactum effugiat: ita enim sese substrahit, ut propemodum seipsam movere videatur.

6. John of Wales, *Summa Justitiae*, London, British Library MS Harley 632, fol. 217v: "Item secundum alios, Accidia est tristicia vel tedium boni spiritualis deo debiti." Cited by Siegfrid Wenzel (170) and translated from the Latin.

7. John of Wales, fol. 217r: "Sequitur de tribus residuis quibus deformatur etiam homo exterior, viz., de accidia, gula, et luxuria. Accidia enim pro parte ad corpus pertinere videtur. Crisostomus, Homilia 18 impefecta: 'Tres sunt precipue

passiones naturales intime et proprie carnis. Primo esca et potus, deinde amor viri ad mulierem, tertio loco sompnus.'" Cited by Wenzel (171) and translated.

8. David of Augsburg, *Formula novitiorum. De interioris hominis reformatione,* 50 (Bigne, XIII, 437). Cited by Wenzel, 180.

9. David of Augsburg, cited by Wenzel, 160.

10. My attention was drawn to the Troilus reference by Ian Bishop's *Troilus and Criseyde: A Critical Study,* 93.

11. John Marston, *Satire II, Works* 3.276.147–49.

Notes to Chapter 5

1. Cited by John Dover Wilson, 310, from *Shakespeare Jahrbuch* (1896). See also Mary I. O'Sullivan, 667.

2. Cited by Wilson, 310, from Dowden's 1899 edition of *Hamlet.*

3. O'Sullivan, 677–78. She refers to Bright's characterization of the melancholy man as "doubtfull before, and long in deliberation: suspicious, painefull in studie, and circumspect" (*Treatise,* 124); his "resolution riseth of long deliberation, because of doubt and distrust" (131). Bright also says of melancholy persons that their "sorrowfull humour breedeth in them. . . . a negligence in their affaires, and dissoluteness, where should be diligence" (135), that "contemplations are more familiar with melancholicke persons then with other, by reason they be not so apt for action" (200), and that "while their passions be not yet vehement," yet "the vehemencie of theyr affection once raysed. . . . carieth them. . . . into the deapth of that they take pleasure to intermeddle in" (130).

4. G. B. Harrison, introduction to *Hamlet,* 881.

5. This identification was first made by S. Puckle, *Funeral Customs: Their Origins and Development;* cited in Roland Mushat Frye, *The Renaissance Hamlet,* 96.

6. The copy I read contained two signatures: William Lawrence, Brasenose College, Oxford, 1703 and Daniel Harris, Magdalene College, Cambridge, 1710–11.

7. Ernest Jones, *Hamlet and Oedipus,* 92–93. This is a revision of an essay published in 1910 in the *American Journal of Psychology* and in 1923 as the first chapter of the author's *Essays in Applied Psychoanalysis.*

8. Erik H. Erikson, "Youth: Fidelity and Diversity," 5–27. Cited by Norman Holland, 174.

BIBLIOGRAPHY

Ackerman, J. C. Introduction to volume XVI, *Opera Claudii Galeni.* In *Medicorum Graecorum Opera Quae Exstant,* xcviii–c. Edited by D. Carolus Gottlob Kühn. Lipsiae: Libraria Carolus Cnoblochii, 1821.

Aers, David. *Chaucer, Langland and the Creative Imagination.* London: Routledge & Kegan Paul, 1980.

Altschule, Mark D. *"Acedia: its evolution from deadly sin to psychiatric syndrome." British Journal of Psychiatry* 3, no. 471 (1965): 117–19.

Anderson, Ruth L. *Elizabethan Psychology and Shakespeare's Plays.* 1927. Reprint. New York: Russell & Russell, 1966.

Andreas Capellanus. *The Art of Courtly Love.* Trans. John Jay Parry. New York: Frederick Unger, 1957.

Anonymous [initialed M. D.] *Notes and Queries* 7 (1853): 546.

Aretaeus, the Cappadocian. *On the Causes and Symptoms of Chronic Diseases, The Extant Works of Aretaeus.* Edited and translated by Francis Adams. London: Wertheimer and Co., 1856.

Arnaldus de Villanova. *Opera.* Lyons: Franciscum Fraden, 1509. New York Academy of Medicine.

———. "Tractatus De Amore Heroico." Edited by Michael R. McVaugh. In *Opera Medica Omnia,* III. Barcelona: Universidad de Barcelona, 1985.

Avicenna. *Liber Canonis De Medicinis.* Venice: Petrus Maufer, 1486. New York Academy of Medicine.

———. *Liber Canonis De Medicinis.* Translated by Gerardo Carmonensi postea uero aba Andrea Alpago. Basiliae, 1556. New York Academy of Medicine.

———. *Liber Canonis De Medicinis.* Translated by Andreas

Alpagus. Venetiis [Venice]: Junta, 1562. New York Academy of Medicine.

————. "A Treatise on Love by Ibn Sina," Trans. Emil L. Fackenheim. *Mediaeval Studies* 7(1945): 208–28.

Babb, Lawrence. *The Elizabethan Malady*. East Lansing, Michigan: Michigan State University Press, 1951.

Baker, Donald C. "Imagery and Structure in Chaucer's *Book of the Duchess*." *Studia Neophilogus*, 30 (1958): 17–26.

Beccaria, Augusto. *I Codici Di Medicina Del Periodo Presalernitano: Secoli IX, X and XI*. Roma: Edizioni Di Storia e Letteratura, 1956.

Bennett, J. A. W. *Chaucer at Oxford and at Cambridge*. Oxford, England: Oxford University Press, 1974.

Bennett, Robert B. "The Reform of a Malcontent: Jaques and the Meaning of *As You Like It*." *Shakespeare Studies* 9 (1976): 183–204.

Bernard of Gordon. [Bernardus Gordonius.] *Omnium Aegritudinem a Vertice ad Calcem, Opus Praeclarissimus quod Lilium Medicinae*. Paris: Gualtherot, 1542. New York Academy of Medicine.

Benton, John. "Clio and Venus: An Historical View of Medieval Love." In *The Meaning of Courtly Love*, 19–41. Edited by F. X. Newman. Albany, New York: State University of New York Press, 1969.

Bettelheim, Bruno. *The Uses of Enchantment*. New York: Vintage Books, 1977.

Biesterfeldt, Hans and Dimitri Gutas. "The Malady of Love." *Journal of the American Oriental Society* 104 (1984): 12–22.

Bishop, Ian. *Troilus and Criseyde: A Critical Study*. Bristol, England: University of Bristol, 1981.

Boase, Roger. *The Origin and Meaning of Courtly Love*. Manchester, England: Manchester University Press, 1977.

Boorde, Andrew. *The Breviarie of Health*. London: Thomas East, 1587. New York Academy of Medicine.

Bradley, A. C. *Shakespearean Tragedy*. 1905. Reprint. New York: Meridian Books, 1955.

Bright, Timothy. *A Treatise of Melancholie*. New York: Columbia University Press for the Facsimile Text Society, 1940.

Bucknill, John Charles. *The Mad Folk of Shakespeare*. 1867. Reprint. New York: Burt Franklin, 1969.

Bucknill, John Charles and Daniel H. Tuke. *A Manual of Psychological Medicine*. Philadelphia: Blanchard and Lea, 1858.

Bundy, Murray W. "Shakespeare and the Elizabethan Psychology." *Journal of English and Germanic Philology* 23 (1924): 516–49.

Burlin, Robert B. *Chaucerian Fiction.* Princeton, New Jersey: Princeton University Press, 1977.

Burrow, John A. *The Ages of Man: A Study in Medieval Writing and Thought.* Oxford: Clarendon Press, 1986.

Burton, Robert. *The Anatomy of Melancholy.* Edited by Floyd Dell and Paul Jordan-Smith. New York: Tudor Publishing Co., 1948.

―――. *The Anatomy of Melancholy.* Edited by Holbrook Jackson. New York: Vintage Books, 1977.

Caelius Aurelianus. *On Acute Diseases and on Chronic Diseases.* Edited and translated by I. E. Drabkin. Chicago: University of Chicago Press, 1950.

Calendar of the Patent Rolls Preserved in the Public Record Office Prepared Under the Superintendence of the Deputy Keeper of the Records, Richard II, A.D. *1385–1389.* London: Printed for Her Majesty's Stationery Office by the Norfolk Chronicle Company, Ltd., Norwich, 1900.

Campbell, Lily B. *Shakespeare's Tragic Heroes: Slaves of Passion.* 1930. Reprint. New York: Barnes & Noble, 1965.

Charron, Pierre. *Of Wisdome.* Trans. S. Lennard. London: 1625. New York Public Library.

Chaucer, Geoffrey. *The Riverside Chaucer.* Gen. ed. Larry D. Benson. 3rd ed. Boston: Houghton Mifflin, 1987.

Cholmeley, H. P. *John of Gaddesden and the Rosa Medicinae.* Oxford: Clarendon Press, 1912.

Ciavolella, Massimo. *La "Malattia D'Amore" dall'Antichità al Medioevo.* Rome: Bulzoni, 1976.

Clemen, Wolfgang. *Chaucer's Early Poetry.* London: 1963.

Coleridge, Samuel T. *Coleridge's Essays and Lectures on Shakespeare.* Edited by Ernest Rhys. London: J. M. Dent, 1909.

Constantinus Africanus. *De Coitu.* Translated by S. Delany. *Chaucer Review* 4 (1970): 55–65.

―――. Liber *de Oblivione.* In Isaac Judaeus, *Omnia Opera.* Leyden: Bartholomeus Trot, 1515. New York Academy of Medicine.

―――. *Opera.* Basle, 1536. New York Academy of Medicine.

Craig, Hardin. Introduction to *As You Like It.* In *The Complete Works of Shakespeare.* Edited by Hardin Craig. Chicago, Illinois: Scott, Foresman, and Co., 1961. 586–88.

Cuffe, Henry. *The Differences of the Ages of Man's Life.* London: Arnold Hatfield for Martin Clearke, 1607.

Curry, Walter Clyde. *Chaucer and the Mediaeval Sciences.* 1926; New York: Barnes and Noble, 1960.

Dante Alighieri. *The Divine Comedy.* Translated and edited by Charles Singleton. 6 vols. Princeton, New Jersey: Princeton Univ. Press, 1973–89.

Demaitre, Luke E. *Doctor Bernard de Gordon: Professor and Practitioner.* Toronto: Pontifical Institute of Mediaeva Studies, 1980.

Denomy, C. S. B., Alexander J. "Concerning the Accessibility of Arabic Influence to the Earliest Troubadours." *Mediaeval Studies*, 15 (1953): 147–58.

———. "*Fin' Amors*: The Pure Love of the Troubadours, its Amorality, and Possible Source." *Mediaeval Studies* 7 (1945). 189–205.

———. *The Heresy of Courtly Love.* Gloucester, Mass.: Peter Smith, 1965.

Donaldson, E. Talbot. "The Ending of Chaucer's *Troilus*." In *Speaking of Chaucer*, 84–101. New York: W. W. Norton, 1970.

———. "The Myth of Courtly Love." In *Speaking of Chaucer*, 154–63. New York: W. W. Norton, 1970.

———. *The Swan at the Well: Shakespeare Reading Chaucer.* New Haven: Yale University Press, 1985.

Doob, Penelope B. R. *Nebuchadnezzar's Children: Conventions of Madness in Middle English Literature.* New Haven, Conn.: Yale University Press, 1974.

Dove, Mary. *The Perfect Age of Man's Life.* Cambridge: Cambridge University Press, 1986.

Du Laurens, André. *Of Melancholie Diseases and of the Meanes to Cure Them.* Translated by Richard Surphlet. London: Felix Kingston for Ralph Iacson, 1599.

Edgar, Irving I. "Shakespeare's Hamlet and the 'melancholy' of the Sixteenth Century." *Psychiatric Quarterly Supplement* 32 (1958): 68–75.

Edwards, Robert R. *The Dream of Chaucer: Representation and Reflection in the Early Narratives.* Durham, North Carolina: Duke University Press, 1989.

Elyot, Sir Thomas. *The Castell of Health.* London: Widdow Orwin & Matthew Lawnes, 1595. The New York Academy of Medicine.

Erikson, Erik H. "Youth: Fidelity and Diversity." *Daedalus* 91 (1962). 5–27.

Ferrand, Jacques. *A Treatise on Lovesickness/Jacques Ferrand.* Translated and edited by Massimo Ciavolella and Donald Beecher. Syracuse, New York: Syracuse University Press, 1990.

Ferrand, James [sic.] *Erotomania or A Treatise Discoursing of the Essence, Causes, Symptoms, Prognostics, and cure of Love.* Oxford, England: L. Lichfield, 1640. Houghton Library, Harvard University.

Foucault, Michel. *Madness and Civilization: A History of Insanity in the Age of Reason.* Translated by Richard Howard. New York: Vintage Books, 1973.

Freud, Sigmund. *The Interpretation of Dreams.* Translated by A. A. Brill. London: G. Allen & Unwin, 1915.

―――. "Mourning and Melancholia." In *Collected Papers* IV, Papers on Metapsychology, 152–70. London: Hogarth Press and the Institute for Psychoanalysis, 1924–50.

Friedman, John B. "The Dreamer, the Whelp, and Consolation in *The Book of the Duchess.*" *Chaucer Review* 3 (1969): 145–62.

Frye, Northrop. *A Natural Perspective.* New York: Harcourt, 1965.

Frye, Roland Mushat. *The Renaissance Hamlet: Issues and Responses in 1600.* Princeton: Princeton University Press, 1984.

Galen. *On the Affected Parts.* Translated and edited by Rudolph E. Siegel. Basel: S. Karger, 1976.

Gardner, Helen. "As You Like It." In *Twentieth-Century Interpretations of "As You Like It,"* 55–69. Edited by Jay L. Halio. Englewood Cliffs, N.J.: Prentice Hall, 1968.

The Gouernayle of Helthe with The Medecyne of Ye Stomache. Reprinted from Caxton's 1489 ed. Introduction and notes by William Blades. London: Blades, East & Blades, 1858.

Greenblatt, Stephen. *Renaissance Self-Fashioning: From More to Shakespeare.* Chicago: University of Chicago Press, 1980.

―――. *Shakespearean Negotiations: The Circulation of Social Energy in Renaissance England.* Berkeley: University of California Press, 1988.

Greene, Robert. *The Repentance of Robert Greene.* In *The Bodley Head Quartos,* vol. 6. Edited by G. B. Harrison. 1923. Reprint. Westport, Conn.: Greenwood Press, 1970.

Grennen, Joseph. "*Hert-Huntyng* in the *Book of the Duchess.*" *Modern Language Quarterly* 25 (1964): 131–39.

Halio, Jay L. "'No Clock in the Forest': Time in *As You Like It.*" *Studies in English Literature, 1500–1900,* 2 (Spring, 1962): 197–207.

Haly Abbas. *Liber Totius Medicine.* Lyons: Michaele de Capella, 1523. New York Academy of Medicine.

―――. *Libri Duo De Melancholia.* Edited by Karl Garbers. Hamburg: Buske, 1977.

Hankins, John E. *The Character of Hamlet and Other Essays.* Chapel Hill, North Carolina: The University of North Carolina Press, 1941.

Harrison, G. B. "Introduction to *Hamlet.*" In *Shakespeare: The*

Complete Works. New York: Harcourt, Brace & World, 1952. 880–84.

Heffernan, Carol Falvo. "Chaucer's *Troilus and Criseyde*: The Disease of Love and Courtly Love." *Neophilologus* 74 (1990): 294–309.

———. "That Dog Again: *Melancholia Canina* and Chaucer's *Book of the Duchess*." *Modern Philology* 84 (1986): 185–90.

———. "Contraception and the Pear Tree Episode of Chaucer's *Merchant's Tale*," *Journal of English and Germanic Philology* 94 (1995): 31–41.

Heiberg, J. L., ed. *Pauli Aeginetae Libri Tertii Interpretatio Latina Antiqua*. Leipzig: Teubner, 1912.

Hill, John M. "*The Book of the Duchess*, Melancholy, and that Eight-Year Sickness." *Chaucer Review* 9 (1974): 35–50.

Hippocrates. *Works*. Edited and translated by W. H. S. Jones. 6 vols. New York: Loeb Classical Library, 1923–88.

Holland, Norman. *Psychoanalysis and Shakespeare*. New York: Octagon Books, 1979.

Jackson, Stanley W. *Melancholia and Depression* . New Haven and London: Yale Univ. Press, 1986.

Jacquart, Danielle and Claude Thomasset. *Sexuality and Medicine in the Middle Ages*. Princeton: Princeton University Press, 1988.

Johannes Anglicus de Gaddesden. *Rosa Anglica Practica Medicine*. Venice, 1492. New York Academy of Medicine.

John of Trevisa. *On the Properties of Things: John of Trevisa's translation of Bartholomaeus Anglicus De Proprietatibus Rerum*. Edited by Michael C. Seymour *et al*. 2 vols. Oxford: Clarendon Press, 1975.

John of Wales. *Summa Justitiae*. MS Harley 632. British Library.

Jones, Ernest. *Hamlet and Oedipus*. Garden City, New York: Doubleday & Co., 1954.

Jordan, Robert M. *Chaucer's Poetics and the Modern Reader*. Berkeley: University of California Press, 1987.

Jorgensen, Paul. "Hamlet's Therapy." *Huntington Library Quarterly* 27 (1964): 239–58.

Juan Huarte de San Juan. *Examen de Ingenios*. Translated by Richard Carew. London, 1594. New York Academy of Medicine.

Juan Huarte de San Juan. *Examen de ingenios: or, the tryal of wits, made English. by Edward Bellamy*. London: Richard Sore, 1598. New York Academy of Medicine.

Kellogg, A. O. *Shakespeare's Delineations of Insanity, Imbecility, and Suicide*. New York: Hurd and Houghton, 1866.

Keynes, Geoffrey. *Dr. Timothie Bright, 1550–1615: A Survey of his Life with a Bibliography of his Writings.* London: The Wellcome Historical Medical Library, 1962.

Kimbrough, Robert. *Shakespeare's Troilus and Cressida and Its Setting.* Cambridge: Harvard University Press, 1964.

Kirsch, Arthur. "Hamlet's Grief." In *Hamlet*, 122–38. Edited by Harold Bloom. New York: Chelsea House, 1990.

Kittredge, George Lyman. *Chaucer and his Poetry.* Cambridge, Mass.: Harvard University Press, 1915.

Klibansky, Raymond, Erwin Panofsky, and Fritz Saxl. *Saturn and Melancholy.* New York: Nelson, 1964.

Lacan, Jacques. "Desire and the Interpretation of Desire in *Hamlet.*" In *Literature and Psychoanalysis*, 11–52. Edited by Shoshana Felman. Baltimore: Johns Hopkins University Press, 1982.

Levinius Lemnius. *The Touchstone of Complexions.* "Englished" by Thomas Newton. London: Thomas Barth, 1576. New York Academy of Medicine.

Lewis, C. S. *The Allegory of Love.* New York: Oxford University Press, 1958.

Loomis, Roger S. "Chaucer's Eight Years' Sickness." *Modern Language Notes* 59 (1944): 178–80.

Lowes, John Livingston. "The Loveres Maladye of Hereos." *Modern Philology* 11 (1914): 4.491–546.

Lyons, Bridget Gellert. *Voices of Melancholy: Studies in Literary Treatments of Melancholy in Renaissance England.* New York: Barnes & Noble, 1971 .

MacDonald, Michael. *Mystical Bedlam: Madness, Anxiety, and Healing in Seventeenth-Century England.* Cambridge, England: Cambridge University Press, 1981.

Mann, Jill. *Medieval Estates Satire.* Cambridge, England: Cambridge University Press, 1973.

Marlowe, Christopher. *The Complete Works of Christopher Marlowe.* Edited by Fredson Bowers. 2nd ed. 2 vols. Cambridge, England: Cambridge University Press, 1981.

Marston, John. *The Works of John Marston.* Edited by Arthur Henry Bullen. 3 vols. London: John C. Nimmo, 1887.

Menocal, Maria Rosa. *The Arabic Role in Medieval Literary History: A Forgotten Heritage.* Philadelphia: University of Pennsylvania Press, 1987.

Milton, John. *Complete Poems and Major Prose.* Edited by Merrit Y. Hughes. New York: The Odyssey Press, 1957.

Mitchell, Jerome. *Thomas Hoccleve: A Study in Early Fifteenth-Century English Poetic.* Urbana, Illinois: University of Illinois Press, 1968.

Muscatine, Charles. "Chaucer's religion and the Chaucer religion." In *Chaucer Traditions: Studies in Honour of Derek Brewer,* Edited by Ruth Morse and Barry Windeatt. Cambridge, England: Cambridge University Press, 1990.

Nash, Thomas. *Works.* Edited by R. B. McKerrow and revised by F. P. Wilson. 5 vols. 1904. Reprint. Oxford: Basil Blackwell, 1958.

Neaman, Judith. "Brain Physiology and Poetics in *The Book of the Duchess.*" *Res Publica Litterarum* 1 (1980): 101–13.

Nykl, A. R. *The Dove's Neck-Ring.* Paris: P. Geuthner, 1931.

———. *Hispano-Arabic Poetry and Its Relations with the Old Provencal Troubadours.* Baltimore: J. H. Furst Co., 1946.

Olson, Glending. *Literature as Recreation in the Later Middle Ages.* Ithaca, New York: Cornell University Press, 1982.

Oribasius. *Synopseos ad Evastathium Filium Libri Novem.* Venice: Paulum Manutium, Aldi Filium, 1554. New York Academy of Medicine.

O'Sullivan, Mary I. "Hamlet and Dr. Timothy Bright." *Publications of the Modern Language Association* 41 (1926): 667–79.

Otten, Charlotte, ed. *A Lycanthropy Reader: Werewolves in Western Culture.* Syracuse, New York: Syracuse University Press, 1986.

Ovid. *The Metamorphoses.* Trans. Frank Justus Miller. London: William Heinemann, 1929.

Panofsky, Erwin. *Albrecht Dürer.* Princeton: Princeton University Press, 1948.

Paracelsus. *Four Treatises of Theophrastus von Hohenheim called Paracelsus.* Trans. C. Lilian Temkin, George Rosen, Gregory Zilboorg, Henry E. Sigerist. Edited and Preface by Henry E. Sigerist. Baltimore: The Johns Hopkins Press, 1941.

Patterson, Lee. *Negotiating the Past: The Historical Understanding of Medieval Literature.* Madison, Wisconsin: The University of Wisconsin, 1987.

Paul of Aegina. *The Seven Books of Paulus Aegineta.* Translated and edited by Francis Adams. London: C. and J. Adlard, 1844.

Pigeaud, Jackie. *La Maladie de L'Âme: Étude sur la relation de l'âme et du corps dans la tradition medico-philosophique antique.* Paris: Société D'Edition "Les Belles Lettres," 1981.

Platter, Felix. "Praxeos." In *Animi Commotio, Observationum. Libri tres.* Basel, 1641. New York Academy of Medicine.

Rhazes. *Opera Parva.* Venice, 1537. New York Academy of Medicine.

Rhazes. *Continens . . . ordinatus & Correctus per . . . Hieronymous*

Surinanus. Venice [Bernardinus Benalius], 1509. New York Academy of Medicine.

———. *Liber Almansoris.* Klebs, no. 8263. Venice: 1500. Reprint of the 1497 edition. New York Academy of Medicine.

Richardson, William. *A Philosophical Analysis and Illustration of Some of Shakespeare's Remarkable Characters.* 3rd ed. London: J. Murray, 1784.

Robbins, Rossell Hope. "The Physician's Authorities." In *Studies in Language and Literature in Honor of Margaret Schlauch,* 335–41. Edited by M. Brahmer et al. Warsaw: Polish Scientific Publishers, 1966.

Robertson, Jr., D. W. and Bernard F. Huppé. *Fruyt and Chaf: Studies in Chaucer's Allegories.* Princeton, New Jersey: Princeton University Press, 1963.

Robertson, Jr., D. W. *A Preface to Chaucer: Studies in Medieval Perspectives.* Princeton, New Jersey: Princeton University Press, 1962

Robinson, F. N. "Explanatory Notes" to *The Book of the Duchess. The Works of Geoffrey Chaucer,* 773–78. Ed. F. N. Robinson. 2nd ed. Boston: Houghton Mifflin Co., 1957.

Sadler, Lynn V. "Chaucer's *The Book of the Duchess* and the 'Lawe of Kinde'." *Annuale Mediaevale* 11 (1970): 51–64.

Salter, Elizabeth. "*Troilus and Criseyde:* A Reconsideration." In *Patterns of Love and Courtesy,* 86–106. Edited by J. Lawlor. Evanston, Ill.: Northwestern University Press, 1966.

Sarton, George. "Lilium Medicinae." In *Mediaeval Studies in Honor of J. D. M. Ford.* 239–56. Edited by U. T. Holmes and A. J. Denomy. Cambridge, Mass.: Harvard University Press, 1948.

Schleiner, Winfried . "Jaques and the Melancholy Stag." *English Language Notes* 17 (1980): 175–79.

Schiesari, Juliana. *The Gendering of Melancholia.* Ithaca, New York: Cornell University Press, 1992.

Schücking, Levin L. *The Meaning of Hamlet.* Translated by Graham Rawson. 1937. Reprint. New York: Barnes & Noble, 1966.

Scott, William I. D. *Shakespeare's Melancholics.* London: Mills & Boon, 1962.

Sears, Elizabeth. *The Ages of Man: Medieval Interpretations of the Life Cycle.* Princeton: Princeton University Press, 1986.

Shakespeare, William. *The New Variorum Troilus and Cressida.* Edited by H. N. Hillebrand. Philadelphia: Lippincott, 1953.

———. *The Riverside Shakespeare.* G. Blakemore Evans, *et al.* Boston: Houghton Mifflin, 1974.

Sharpe, Ella Freeman. "The Impatience of Hamlet." In

Collected Papers on Psycho-Analysis, 203–13. Edited by Marjorie Brierly. The International Psychoanalytic Library, No. 36. London: The Hogarth Press, 1952.

Shaw, William P. "Sense and Staging in Shakespeare's Comedies: Jaques and [the] Wedding Dance." In *The Laurel Bough*, 25–33. Edited by G. Nageswara Rao. Bombay: Blackie & Son, 1983.

Shoaf, R. A. *"Mutatio Amoris"*: 'Penitentia' and the Form of *The Book of the Duchess."* *Genre* 14 (1981): 163–89.

Simon, Bennett. *Mind and Madness in Ancient Greece*. Ithaca, New York: Cornell University Press, 1978.

Siraisi, Nancy. *Avicenna in Renaissance Italy: The Canon and Medical Teaching in Italian Universities after 1500*. Princeton: Princeton University Press, 1987.

Spearing, A. C. *Readings in Medieval Poetry*. Cambridge, England: Cambridge University Press, 1987.

Spevack, Marvin. *The Harvard Concordance to Shakespeare*. Cambridge, Massachusetts: Harvard University Press, 1974.

Stern, Samuel M. *Hispano-Arabic Strophic Poetry: Studies*. Edited by L. P. Harvey. Oxford: Clarendon Press, 1974.

Talbot, Charles H. "Medicine." In *Science in the Middle Ages*, 391–428. Edited by David C. Lindberg. Chicago: The University of Chicago Press, 1978.

Tellenbach, Hubertus. *Melancholy: History of the Problem, Endogeneity, Typology, Pathogenesis, Clinical Considerations*. Translated by Erling Eng. Pittsburgh: Duquesne University Press, 1980.

Tractatus de regimine sanitatis virorum spiritualium ac devotorum. Edited by Manfred P. Köch. In *Das "Erfurter Kartauserregimen": Studien zur diatetischen Literatur des Mittelalters*, Dissertation. Bonn, 1969.

"Traites d'hygiene du môyen age." Edited by Leopold Delisle. *Journal des savants* (1896): 518–40.

Ulmann, Manfred. *Islamic Surveys*, Translated by Jean Watt. Edinburgh: Edinburgh University Press, 1978.

Ussery, Huling E. *Chaucer's Physician: Medicine and Literature in Fourteenth-Century England*. Tulane Studies in English, 19. New Orleans, Louisiana: Tulane University Press, 1971.

Valescus de Taranta. *Philonium aurem ac perutile opus practice medicine opera dantibus: quod Philonium appellatur*. Venice, 1521. New York Academy of Medicine.

Wack, Mary F. "The *Liber de heros morbo* of Johannes Afflacius and Its Implications for Medieval Love Conventions." *Speculum* 62 (1987): 324–44.

———. *Love sickness in the Middle Ages: The Viaticum and Its Commentaries.* Philadelphia: University of Pennsylvania Press, 1990.

———. "Lovesickness in *Troilus.*" *Pacific Coast Philology* 19 (1984): 55–61.

———. "New Medieval Medical Texts on *Amor Hereos.*" In *Zusammenhange, Einflusse, Wirkungen,* 288–98. Edited by Joerg O. Fichte et al. Berlin: Walter De Gruyter, 1986.

Wetherbee, Winthrop. *Chaucer and the Poets: An Essay.* Ithaca: Cornell University Press, 1984.

Wenzel, Siegfried. *The Sin of Sloth: Acedia in Medieval Thought and Literature.* Chapel Hill, North Carolina: University of North Carolina, 1960.

Wilhelm, James. *The Cruelest Month: Spring, Nature, and Love in Classical and Medieval Lyrics.* New Haven and London: Yale University Press, 1965.

Wilson, John Dover. *What Happens in Hamlet.* Cambridge, England: Cambridge University Press, 1959.

Wimsatt, James. *Chaucer and the French Love Poets.* Chapel Hill, North Carolina: University of North Carolina Press, 1968.

The Wyse Boke of Maystyr Peers of Salerne. Edited by Carol Falvo Heffernan. Forthcoming in *Manuscripta.*

Young, David. *The Heart's Forest: A Study of Shakespeare's Pastoral Plays.* New Haven, Conn.: Yale University Press, 1972.

INDEX

ABOUT THE AUTHOR

Carol Falvo Heffernan is associate professor of English at Rutgers University and has also been a visiting professor at Trinity College, Dublin, Ireland. She is the author of *The Phoenix at the Fountain: Images of Woman and Eternity in Lactantius's Carmen de Ave Phoenice and the Old English Phoenix* (1988) and *Le Bone Florence of Rome* (1976). Dr. Heffernan received her Ph.D. from New York University, and is a member of the Medieval Academy of America, the New Chaucer Society and the Modern Language Association.